Paul J.

TRADITIONAL AND MODERN JU-JITSU

Foreword

Jujitsu 

America

I have read this book written by Paul Davies and I was impressed with the practicality of the art. Mr. Davies attended my seminars and exhibited to me the efficiency of his techniques, giving me an insight of his repertoire.

I see an amazing parallel in our jujitsu career though we are three decades apart. We believe in updating techniques to meet the demands of today. We are eclectic, willing to learn as well as share with others, and we believe that jujitsu training will make a better person and citizen out of the student.

I highly recommend this book to all martial artists who are willing to better themselves. Mr. Paul Davies loves to teach and this is a wonderful way to learn — through the words of Mr. Davies describing the subtleties of each technique.

Professor Wally Jay

Professor Wally Jay
Jujitsu America Founder
Jujitsu Tenth Dan
Judo Sixth Dan

This book is dedicated to:

Captain J. K. L. Davies M.A.
Mrs M. L. Davies B.A.
and
Squiddy

Peterson House,
Berryhill Industrial Estate, Droitwich, Worcestershire WR9 9BL

Sole World Distributors
Peterson Book Company,
Peterson House,
Berryhill Industrial Estate, Droitwich, Worcestershire WR9 9BL

Printed in England by
Worcestershire Web Offset Ltd,
Northbank, Berryhill Industrial Estate, Droitwich, Worcs. WR9 9BL

Contents

INTRODUCTION

The title of this book describes the main thrust of this work. It discusses the historical origins of Ju-Jutsu, formerly Yawara Jutsu, and reviews some of the component parts fundamental to this martial art.

By use of illustrations (where they best describe and show technique) and sequential photographs (where appropriate) the book clearly demonstrates just what traditional Ju Jutsu is all about. Like any written work, one is limited by certain constraints. Thus, whilst not attempting to be a complete study of Ju Jutsu, this book does give a comprehensive look at the techniques of the traditional side of the "pliable science". Ju Jutsu has been the most prolific martial art in terms of giving birth to other martial arts: Judo, Aikido, plus many styles of Karate owe their origins to Ju Jutsu.

I am firmly of the opinion that Ju Jutsu cannot be reduced to a sport without altering its mode of practice and thus eventually its self defence street capabilities. Many martial arts have put other criteria first, other than self defence and street effectiveness. Certain styles of Ju Jutsu have already deteriorated and diluted their studies away from the true way. Change is inevitable as martial skills are adapted to fit the circumstances of today; some teachers keep their techniques and their approach firmly pointing towards effective street credible self defence and combat criteria, some do not.

The tradition of a 'Jutsu' is a truth or science and as such the truth or science, which was both a killing and subduing art, must be preserved.

Having said realism and effectiveness first, free practice and competition which allows competitive testing of Ju Jutsu associated skills, can be a useful training tool. To be useful they must however reflect the skills associated with a particular art. To date, there has been arguably a gap with regards to a vigorous form of competition which had the physical testing of full contact, was also broad based and without the risk of possible brain damage. In the appendix to this book are two useful free practice or potential competitive sports formats. They can be used by the traditionalist who dislikes the ethos of modern sports competition to test his more advanced students. For the competitive sportsman, these formats have been used successfully in both club and international competition. The details of the governing body which is a non profit making organisation is included in the appendix. They will be happy to advise those wishing to run such a tournament.

The positive side of these formats is that they encourage good body conditioning and test skills associated with Ju Jutsu under a very vigorous scenario with minimal risk of serious injury. When open tournaments have been held to date, Ju Jutsu practitioners have won, proving that if a format truly reflects the basic skills of a particular art that art will normally dominate in such contests, after all you do not get Karate men winning the gold medal at the Olympics for Judo. (NB 3 levels of contact see appendix and rules)

This is not because Judo prevents other arts entering its contests. Rather, it is the format which genuinely test the skills associated with Judo. To date whilst formats have existed they have been arguably an adaption of semi contact Karate encorporating throws. As Ju Jutsu practitioners we surely wish to test skills of Ju Jutsu and without a doubt both Sport Budo/Sport Ju Jutsu and Knockdown Jiudo fulfill this aim.

"You get good at what you practice," and when I started Ju Jutsu the aim I had in mind was self defence. Thus as these free practice formats test basic skills associated with self defence, they present the problem of aesthetic or gymnastic criteria overriding self defence considerations in your training. However like any tool they are as useful as the craftsperson who uses them. Competition or free practice to allow testing of certain skills within safe parameters has its place in a Ju Jutsu students development. However if the sport side of an art is allowed to become too important it will inevitably dilute the real "Jutsu" as training for competition rules excludes or prevents use of certain vital techniques.

In many traditional schools Shia or contesting is restricted to students whose mental and physical attributes allow almost real fighting with sufficient self control to preserve life. No sports format can equal the thrill and the skills of such encounters. However today few are willing to dedicate the time or effort (and conquer ego sufficiently) to partake of such traditional Shia. So let the traditionalist and the sportsman remember that both views have a degree of validity. After all there is more to studying martial arts then collecting trophies. Equally the man who is willing to test his skills in open competition will obviously gain knowledge if the format is a realistic one and his attitude is correct.

On a technical point some individuals regard Ju Jutsu as being a set of prelearnt techniques which one uses against attacks. Equally, controversy reigns concerning stances. Some schools stress the particular use of certain stances in certain situations, other schools do not teach formal stance positions. In this book the fundamental stances of Yawara Ryu are shown being used against actual assaults. After all one must remember you learn a set of moves and set stances in order to eventually learn an automatic way of moving and thus be able to respond to attack in an instinctive manner.

With further reference to the books title Traditional Ju Jutsu, let us briefly state what definition of traditional we are refering to. Traditional in the context of this book refers to a "Jutsu" that is a real martial science or truth. As a result the theme of the book is to state the Traditional and modern Ju Jutsu applies tested knowledge and develops it to meet the changing requirements of the present day. It places real martial art study and effective self defence first, sport or free practice being seen as a useful tool, a supplementary activity to real martial art study, but only if used correctly. After all it must be the Dog which wags the tail, not the tail which wags the Dog."

This traditional combat Ju-Jutsu can never be confused with being a sport that has rules. It can however, and does, allow for limited free practice drills in certain areas of the study only, thus ensuring practicality rules over aesthetic criteria. Schools like Tenjin Shoden Katori Shinto Ryu may be classified as that of Bu Jutsu but they teach techniques of both an armed and unarmed nature. Myamoto Musashi in his work 'Book of Five Rings' mentions how when close in with an enemy, one can thrust ones fist into his face to good effect. He also utilises the shoulder, showing uses of the less refined but affective atemi waza indigenous to Japan and Yawara. The founder of Shindo Muso Ryu Jo Jitsu also refined atemi waza to use in conjunction with his new weapon (Jo). The use of the finger thrusts were also a result of Chinese influence as they became part of the newer Edo period Ju-Jutsu schools syllabi. Some of these new booming schools of Ju-Jutsu kept a firm base of the old combat refined Ju-Jutsu and kept away from more aesthetic considerations. They placed emphasis on weaponry in conjunction with unarmed tactics. Some of the newer more 'fancy' schools added weaponry to their syllabi. However, the latter still in some cases lost their way and moved away from the more effective and true Jutsu or killing/subduing skills that are the core of traditional Ju-Jutsu. Others managed to develop and maintain a realistic approach but these were in the minority.

As many schools became much more formalised and hard practice systems gave way to more ritualised methods it could be argued that the quality of some ryus techniques declined. This technical decline could be said to have taken place hand in hand with the political and social changes which left many individuals who had formerly been engaged in the martial arts without a means of bonefide employment or purpose.

Dr. Kano, when introducing his eclectic art of Jiu do was not seeking solely to turn Ju-Jutsu into a sport; what he wanted was a way of making Jiu do suitable as a form of physical culture and to thus allow it to continue and grow by being suitable for use in educational establishments. He bore witness to his wish to preserve real traditional martial skills by sending many of his special students to study other older martial art sciences. Equally, the Kodokan had its own weapons and special studies sections. Dr. Kano also believed that certain areas were suitable for free practice and that whilst only a limited range of skills could be tested in this way, it still had benefits for the art itself and the individual student. Thus throwing for example, which in traditional Ju-Jutsu or Yawara is effected usually by means of a painful lock or pre throw atemi strike (unless the body movement of an attacker is utilised) could be practised without the utilisation of these methods; the idea being that safe contesting could take place (or as in the early days with limited striking to safe areas) so improving the overall throwing techniques of the students. Dr. Kano, I feel, did recognise that in real conflict the traditional method was superior; however if free practise of the sort mentioned took place in conjunction with the study of the battlefield methods the students overall ability and physical skills would be improved. This view can be backed up by the fact that Dr. Kano included in some of his judo kata techniques directly taken from the battlefield application whilst in armour. Likewise, by free practise the mechanically more efficient methods can be refined having regard to the need for atemi or a lock in a real conflict situation.

D. Kano took most of his throwing techniques from Kito Ryu and his striking and locking from Tenjin Shin Yo' Ryu. This fact can be illustrated by the easy way Gunji Koizumi adapted his Ju-Jutsu to the modern Judo, he had after all had extensive experience of one of the primary schools systems upon which the early Judo was based. Dr. Kano sent Sensei Tominiki to study with Usheba and other students to study specialist arts. He did not want to kill off the older arts but saw Judo as a means of building a universally culturally acceptable system which would act as a bridge between the martial past and the present.

CHAPTER ONE
HISTORY

The term Ju-Jitsu means pliable or gentle science. Too often people classify Ju-Jitsu in very simple terms and forget that arguably it is the oldest of the martial arts. In Japanese mythology the gods Kashina and Kadori were said to have availed themselves of the art to chastise the lawless inhabitants of the eastern provinces. This story pre dates 2500 years ago and therefore tends to disprove the theory that Ju-Jitsu was yet another art that grew out of the spreading Chinese and Indian arts. This is not to say that the Chinese and other Asian countries did not have an influence in the development and refinement of Ju-Jitsu in the latter periods around the Edo period and perhaps even before that date.

Historians sometimes argue incorrectly that Takenouchi Ryu was the core school from which all Ju-Jitsu sprang; however earlier ryu have been proven to exist which utilised "empty hand" techniques in support of their primary studies, that is, weaponry.

The view that any one single school of unarmed attack and defence can be claimed to have initiated Ju-Jitsu is a historically weak argument. E. J. Harrison in his book 'The Art of Ju-Jitsu' states that in his opinion, Ju-Jitsu was the result of entirely Japanese exertions rather than being an art introduced from China. Some historians, who look purely at the surface naming of an art and not at its content, often mistakenly take the growth of Ju-Jitsu schools in the Edo period as being the real formal beginning of the art. As a result, they incorrectly regard Ju-Jitsu as an art dealing with purely unarmed defence to armed or unarmed attack. This view is not one that I agree with and such notable researchers and practitioners of martial arts as the late Don Draeger also thought likewise. He defined Ju-Jitsu as "various armed or unarmed fighting systems that can be applied against armed or unarmed enemies, as a 'no holds barred' type of fighting". Don Draeger goes on to point out the view of Arima that Combat Ju-Jitsu developed from battlefield experience and that the younger ryu which did not have such an origin paid more attention to aesthetic considerations and as a result might be deficient in an actual encounter. Today in both Japan and the West, his view could be said to be correct when one sees the over fancy and flowery techniques that blandly get labelled Ju-Jitsu and yet bear no relation to the original and deadly art.

The school of thought that believes Ju-Jitsu owes much to the Chinese mainland does have some substance but from my own research whilst in the orient, this input was of a contributary rather than an initiating nature. For example, Akyana/Shirobei, a physician went to China to study. He returned having mastered three techniques (te) based on kicking and thrusting plus twenty eight revival techniques (Kassei-Ho). His students gave up due to the paucity of his techniques and their harshness. He returned to meditate and whilst doing so observed how whilst the sturdy cherry tree snapped under the weight of the gathering snow, the willow, by giving way and bending, threw off the snow and survived. This inspiration lead to him founding Honti Yoshin Ryu (Willow Hearted School). The Chinese had without doubt developed Ch'uan'fa "fist method" to a greater extent than the Japanese up to 1600. The Japanese had developed basic atemi (striking vital and vulnerable points of the body) but as their unarmed techniques were predominantly developed in conjunction with weaponry studies, they tended to be more simplistic and arguably more direct. The development of such fist methods in China was in the hands of the monks and commoners. In Japan, atemi was primarily restricted in the Heinian period to the warrior class. As weaponry became refined to such high levels, atemi did not need to be pushed in developmental terms.

Stories exist of monks such as Chen teaching his sophisticated striking techniques to Samurai and many such interchanges will have taken place. Thus the atemi system definitely gained from the Chinese 'fist methods' over a long period of time. In the case of Ju-Jitsu, which developed from non military origins, there is no doubt that the Chinese influence was substantial. This however does not displace the real origins of the unarmed and armed studies generically called Yawara and latterly Ju-Jitsu, which were developed from the experiences of real combat, direct and simple in their origins and application.

Certainly these older origins had extremely harsh training methods and also had a store house of deadly weapons and unarmed techniques to draw from. This type of study continues in a few schools but such study requires extreme dedication and the willingness to train in such a way that one has to give of ones total being, developing correct attitude as well as physical technique.

Judo has changed course dramatically since then; whether Dr. Kano saw the art as primarily an Olympic sport with the larger part of its syllabus no longer utilised in competition is doubtful, although he was certainly in favour of its entry into the Olympics being a member of the Japanese Olympic Committee at this time. Here we can see how certainly the face of Judo as presented to the public reflects only a small portion of its real potential. Many clubs concentrate purely on contest within the limited rules allowed to the exclusion of many manoeuvres and locks. Certainly the areas of free practise within the safe parameters as part of the overall art have been long left behind as an ethic. The tool now runs the craftsman and the sport has swallowed almost all of the potentially wonderful systems so practical for self defence prior to its metamorphosis to a modern olympic sport; perhaps a story that should be remembered before too many martial arts groups rush to gain an olympic place and perhaps lose their martial roots. Certain myths exist concerning contest between Dr. Kano's Kodokwan and other Ju-Jitsu Ryu (schools). It must be pointed out that in fairness to the traditional schools, much of their techniques had to be excluded from use in contest in order to preserve life. Equally, the type of contest (throwing format) utilised was normally only used occasionally as a form of free practise whilst the Kodokan utilised it in the extreme as a major training aid. It was after suffering a defeat at the hands of a school that utilised many ground techniques that Dr. Kano introduced ground work as a primary part of Judo. Equally, certain unemployed Ju-Jitsu men at this time, desperate for money, engaged in contest including against Sumo wrestlers, a feat for those who won, which few modern Judo practitioners could equal.

For those who still study the areas of science such as atemi, my apologies, however statistically you are in the minority but well done for keeping the real Judo alive.

It is interesting to note that Ju-Jitsu reached America and Great Britain via young men who were travelling and inevitably passing on some of their skills. Some of them settled and made a living by professionally teaching Ju-Jitsu and later, in the case of Great Britain, the new Jiu do (later Judo) the 'Gentle Way' of Dr. Kanos eclectic system.

In America, men like Professor Henry S. Okazaki could trace their lineage back to Danzan Ryu (Kodenkan) American first disciples of Ju-Jitsu. In America much of the modern development of Ju-Jitsu owes a great deal to men like Professor Wally Jay, who developed and refined the effective 'small circle theory'! In Great Britain men like S. K. Uyenishi, Gunki Koizumi and Yoko Tani did much to promote Ju-Jitsu. Certain organisations claim to be the only link with these Ju-Jitsu men; however, with a little research one can soon see how in Britain these men had a prolific effect.

My own primary teachers Senseis W. Rankin and R. Lawrence both had experience under the early Japanese Ju-Jitsu teachers. Politics must never be allowed to belittle or destroy this great martial art. If sporting contests are introduced we must learn from the history of Judo. We as Ju-Jitsu men must separate the real martial art from the combat sports. The combat sports must themselves reflect Ju-Jitsu skills not those more commonly associated with other arts. After all, each to their own!

To those who see sport and contest merely as a way of free practise rather than entering in the public arena, we must provide a system for such free practise. To date adequate combat sport formats have existed for Judo and Karate. Sport Budo/Sport Ju-Jitsu is a format which allows very vigorous yet safe contesting. It is designed to minimise the dangers of brain damage whilst keeping the targets and power realistic. In the appendix, the rules for this competitive format plus Knockdown Jiu do (also developed by the writer and used successfully at both club and international competitive level) are laid out. These can be used as a tool for free practise within the club as a part of a training schedule or for those who wish, at competition level. If you wish to compete in this truly Ju-Jitsu orientated sporting format, the address of the International governing body is in the appendix.

The debate about the use of sport and competition will continue for many years. What is certain is that vigorous appropriate practise is necessary for a Ju-Jitsu student to reach his or her full potential. Certain areas of study can be placed within safe parameters. some cannot; however, the traditional side must be preserved whatever road is followed so that Ju-Jitsu can maintain its traditional status, that of a real martial art, a science and a truth.

Before moving onto the fundamentals of Ju-Jitsu, let us quickly look at the historical origins of three techniques used by many practitioners today. By looking at the historical origins, one can analyse why techniques are exercised in a particular way. Likewise, when developing the art one needs occasionally to return to the 'grass roots' and thus ensure development does not detract from tried and tested principles, after all, the human body has changed little.

By maintaining this balance, evolution can take place without the "Jitsu" (Science or Truth) losing it martial base or fighting edge.

One can clearly see these core techniques in today's Ju-Jitsu.

'By knowing ones past, one can better chart the course of ones future! Having reviewed briefly the past, let us now look at the fundamentals of the sciences today known as Ju-Jutsu or Ju-Jitsu.

CHAPTER TWO

FUNDAMENTALS OF JU-JITSU

Different styles or Ju-Jitsu have different component parts.

Let us list the main areas common to the greatest number of Ju-Jitsu systems, sects or styles:

Dachi Waza = stances;
Ukemi Waza = breakfalling;
Atemi Waza = striking;
Nage Waza = throwing;
Ne Waza = ground techniques:
Katame Waza = locking, strangling, choking;
(inclusion of such sub divisions as pressure points and flesh ripping, biting);
Revival techniques;
Strategy;
Weaponry.
(Note: these divisions or sections are for convenience of analysis and may be further sub divided).

It is worth noting that many of the modern Ju-Jitsu schools would be better classified as Goshin Jutsu or Self Defence systems which are simplfied versions of the older more complex systems. Ironically, the early systems as previously mentioned were initially quite primitive and limited in the number of tricks used and yet over the years they grew as new expertise was added. The modern Goshin systems can often be quite small in content allowing the practitioner to gain a degree of expertise and ability within a reasonable time period, rather than the more extensive study required in some of the traditional Ryu. For example, in Tenshin Shoden Katori Shinto Ryu an individual only reaches the top level with constant study after fifteen years. This length of time being somewhat inappropriate for those individuals who wish to learn a self defence system for modern day use and keep fit rather than dedicating their life to the study of martial arts. Having made this point, let us now analyse and show some of the basic techniques in each of those main areas identified as being the fundamentals of Ju-Jitsu generally.

I must point out that because of the miscellaneous sections that each individual school or sect developed, some may feel that their system has parts not defined in the list of fundamentals. Nevertheless, it is fair to say, that the large majority of Ju-Jitsu practitioners will recognise those areas listed as being either part of their study or part of their comrades studies in different schools of Ju-Jitsu.

CHAPTER THREE

ATEMI-WAZA

Atemi-waza can be defined as the art of rendering a person unconscious, dead or incapacitated, by use of specialist strikes to vulnerable areas of the body. Some would define atemi-waza as being the use of the body's natural weapons delivering multiple-strikes to vital and vulnerable spots.

If one looks at the chart (fig. 1) one can see those areas most generally accepted as being vital targets to which atemi can be used.

The methods of atemi vary greatly but as Tenjin Shin Yo Ryu was a school that relied heavily on atemi-waza we will use them as a guide to the usual natural weapons used for striking these specific targets (as illustrated on pages 13, 14, 15 and 16).

Body weapons; (tools of atemi waza).

Head;(a)	Second knuckles;(f)	Finger strikes(j^1/j^2)	Shin;(n)
Shoulders;	Phoenix fist;(g)	Palm heel strike;(k)	Heel;(o)
Elbows; (b^1/b^2)	Thumb;(h)	Eagles claw;(I)	Foot edge;(p)
Forearms; (C^1/C^2)	Fist; (i^a)	Hips;	Ball of foot;(q)
Wrists;(d)	Hammer fist;(i^B)/ Reverse;(i^C)	Knee;(m)	Instep;(r)
Hand edges;(e^1)(e^2)	Back fist;(i^C)		

and many variations on the above list.

It should be noted that the various finger strikes become predominantly part of Ju-Jitsu during the Edo period.

Prior to this, on the battlefield the fist and other striking parts were predominantly used. Miyamoto Musashi, who studied grappling arts as well as his famous two sword system, mentions in his writings 'A Book of Five Rings' a favoured tactic of his when close to an adversary (when both partie's swords were engaged) that thrusting his fist into his antagonists face was a most useful and practical manoeuvre.

This very short list of striking methods can be greatly enlarged if one further subdivides the specific use and the various ways in which the different ryu developed particular types of strikes, for example the middle finger strike-'phoenix fist' as it is often called can be described as a further way of utilising the fist or fingers to render damage to antagonists.

Interestingly, there is a legend about an Indian prince who discovered the vital points later used in acupuncture by taking prisoners and driving needles (and knives) into these different parts of their bodies and recording the results

VITAL STRIKING AREAS (FRONT)

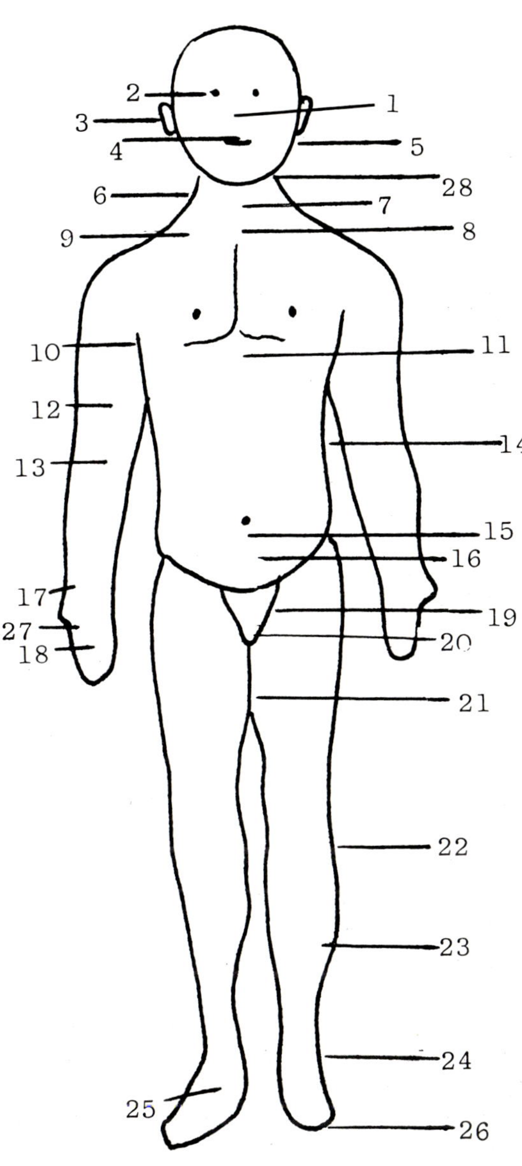

(1) Bridge of nose
(2) eyes
(3) ears
(4) base of nose
(5) mastoid
(6) base of neck
(7) larynx
(8) clavical sternum notch
(9) collar bone
(10) under armpit
(11) solar plexus
(12) below bicep
(13) inside of elbow
(14) base of ribs
(15) hypogastrium
(16) bladder
(17) wrist
(18) base of fingers 3/4
(19) pressure point
(20) groin
(21) femoral (inside thigh)
(22) kneecaps
(23) shin
(24) ankle
(25) instep
(26) toes
(27) between thumb/ 1st finger
(28) jawbone

BACK

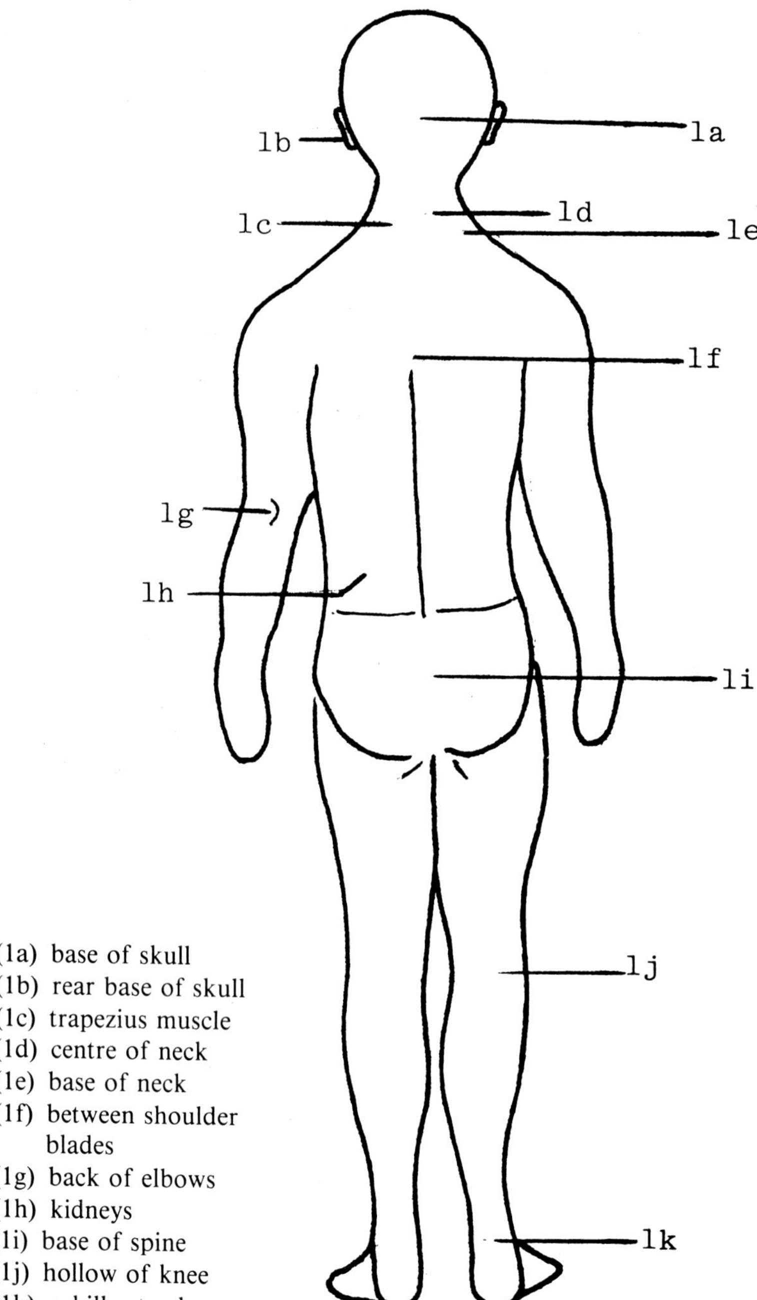

(1a) base of skull
(1b) rear base of skull
(1c) trapezius muscle
(1d) centre of neck
(1e) base of neck
(1f) between shoulder blades
(1g) back of elbows
(1h) kidneys
(1i) base of spine
(1j) hollow of knee
(1k) achilles tendon

that were obtained. Whether this knowledge filtered its way to Japan via China or directly, is not known. Equally, the vital points may have become known to Japanese warriors through their own studies and through their own experience on the battlefield. What is certain is that atemi-waza by virtue of its speed, its multiple strikes and the use of the body as a killing weapon make it a deadly martial science.

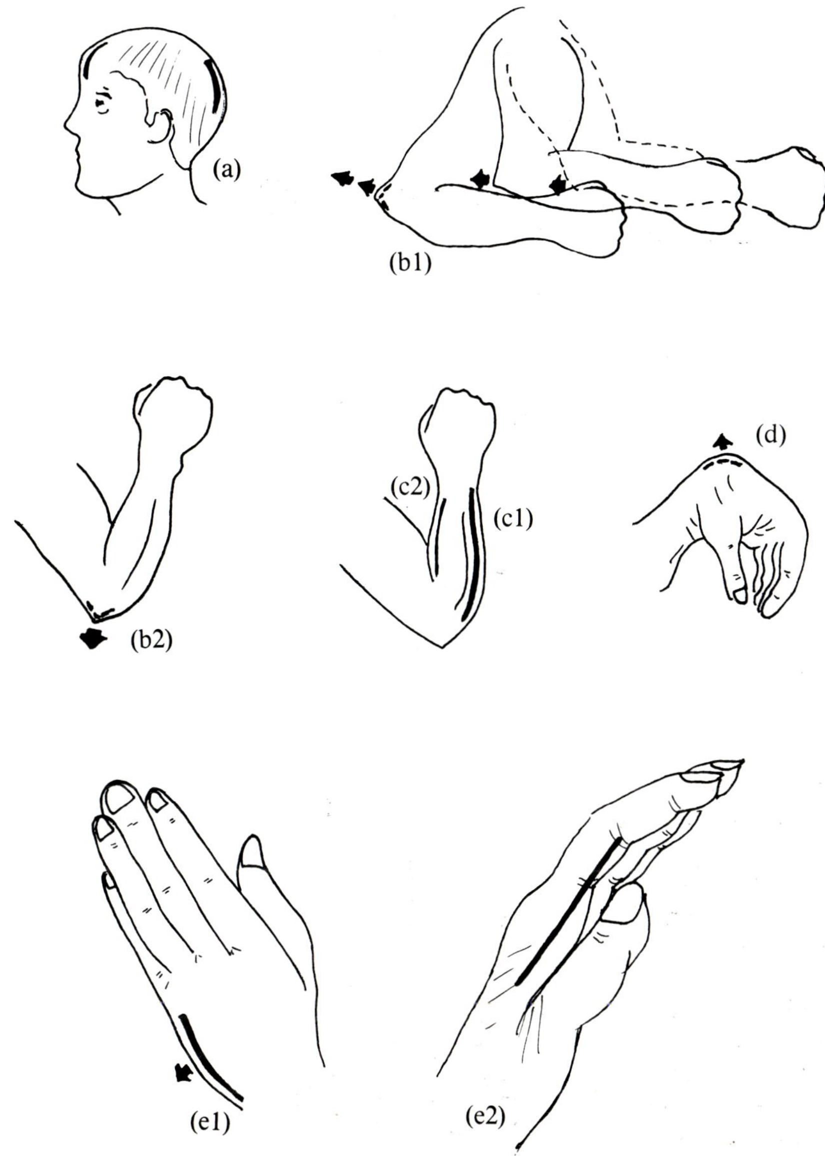

(f)

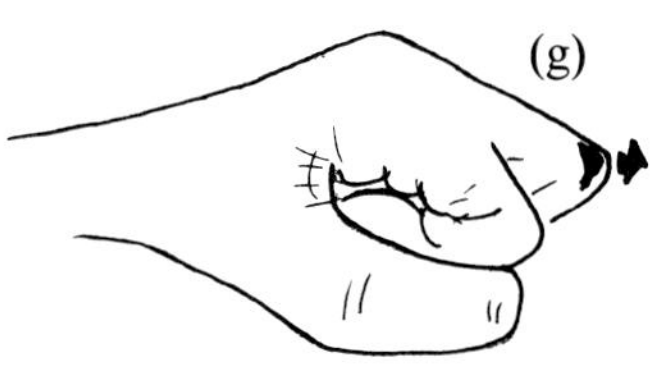
(g)

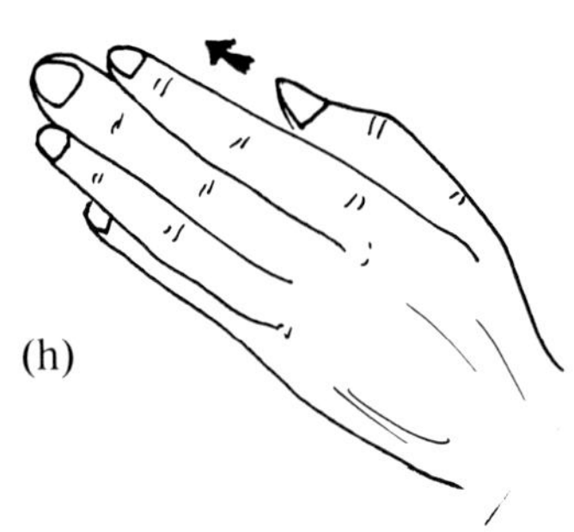
(h)

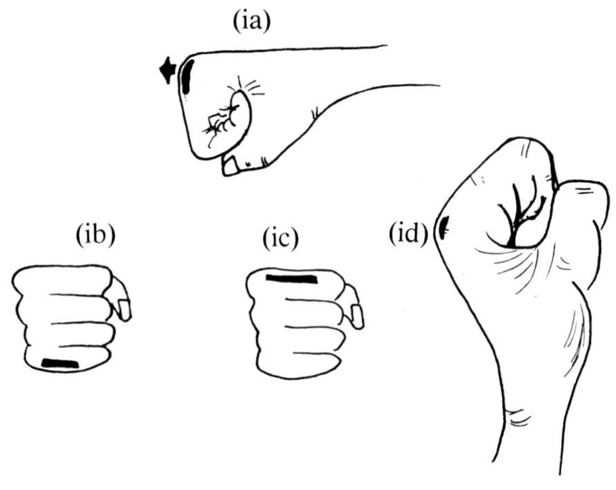
(ia)
(ib)
(ic)
(id)

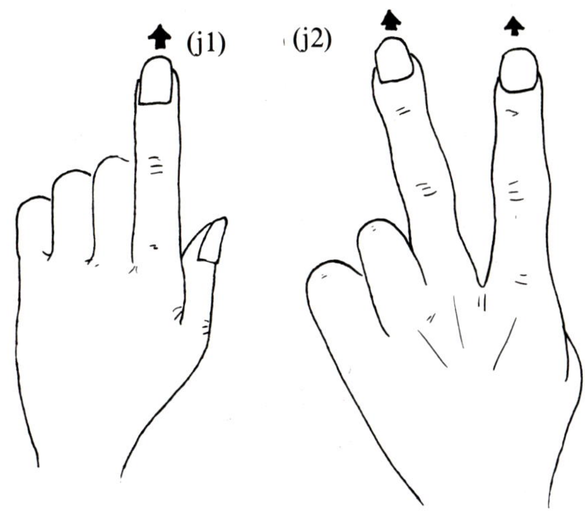
(j1)
(j2)

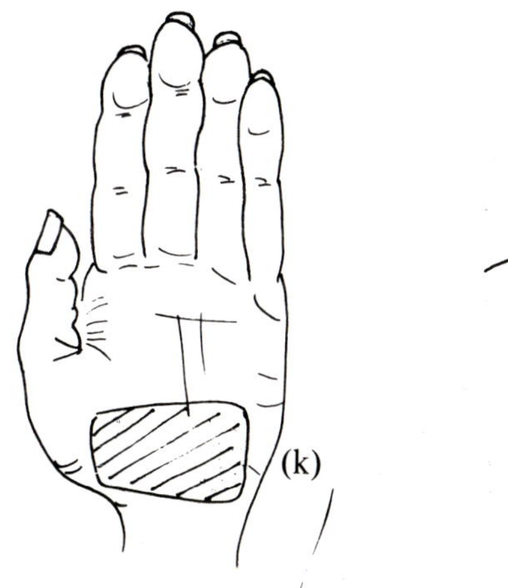
(k)

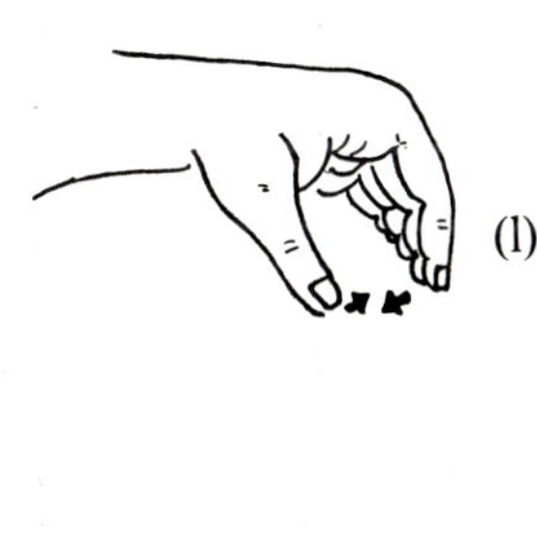
(l)

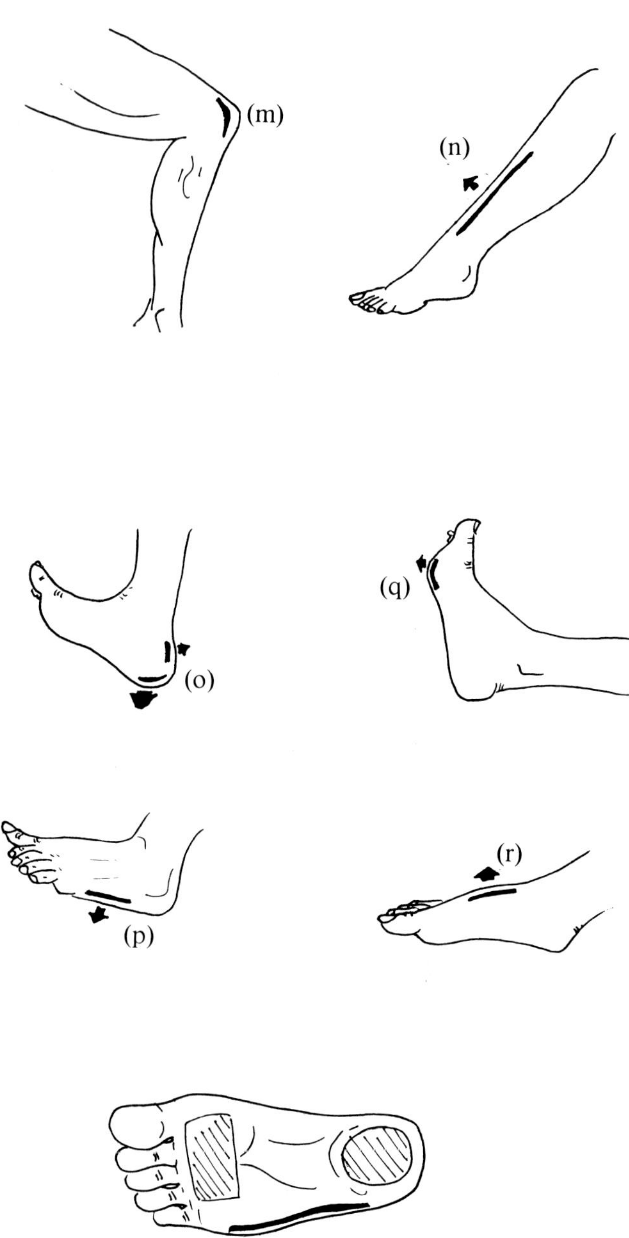
(m)
(n)
(o)
(q)
(p)
(r)

1 KNIFE HAND (SHUTO-UCHI) under the nose.

The attacker attempts a downward type blow, the defender blocks and evades bringing the attacker onto the blow just below the nose. This will cause considerable damage such as a bursting fracture of the upper jaw bone, if executed with sufficient force. Even if lightly struck it will normally cause damage to teeth, lips, etc. (Caution in training when using such technique.)

2 KNIFE HAND (thrusting) to the collar bone.

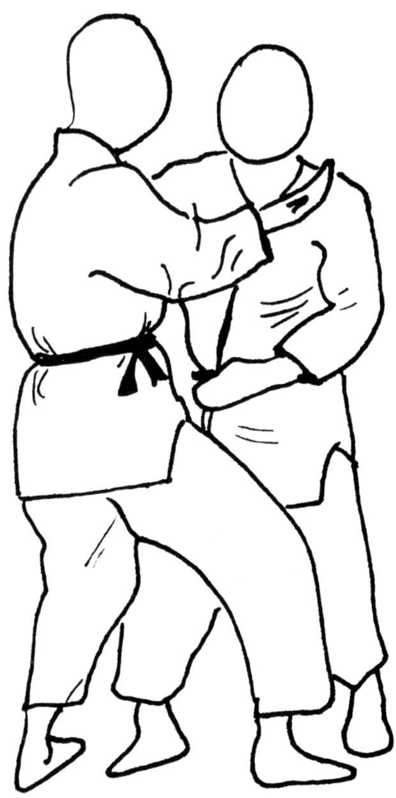

The defender utilises a thrusting knife-hand strike, causing the collar bone to break. Ensure that the strike is focused to the centre of the clavical and that one pushes through with the blow to exacerbate the pain and thus potency of this strike.

3 KNIFE HAND to side of neck.

This technique is one which should be used with caution. Use only a medium force, otherwise the blow in extreme cases causes death by affecting a major nerve associated with the regulation of the heart beat. If you are experienced, your accuracy can allow this strike to be used as an anaethetising strike, but beware of it's use and ensure you avoid striking the vegus nerve too hard.

4 HAMMER FIST (KENTSUI UCHI) to the side of jaw.

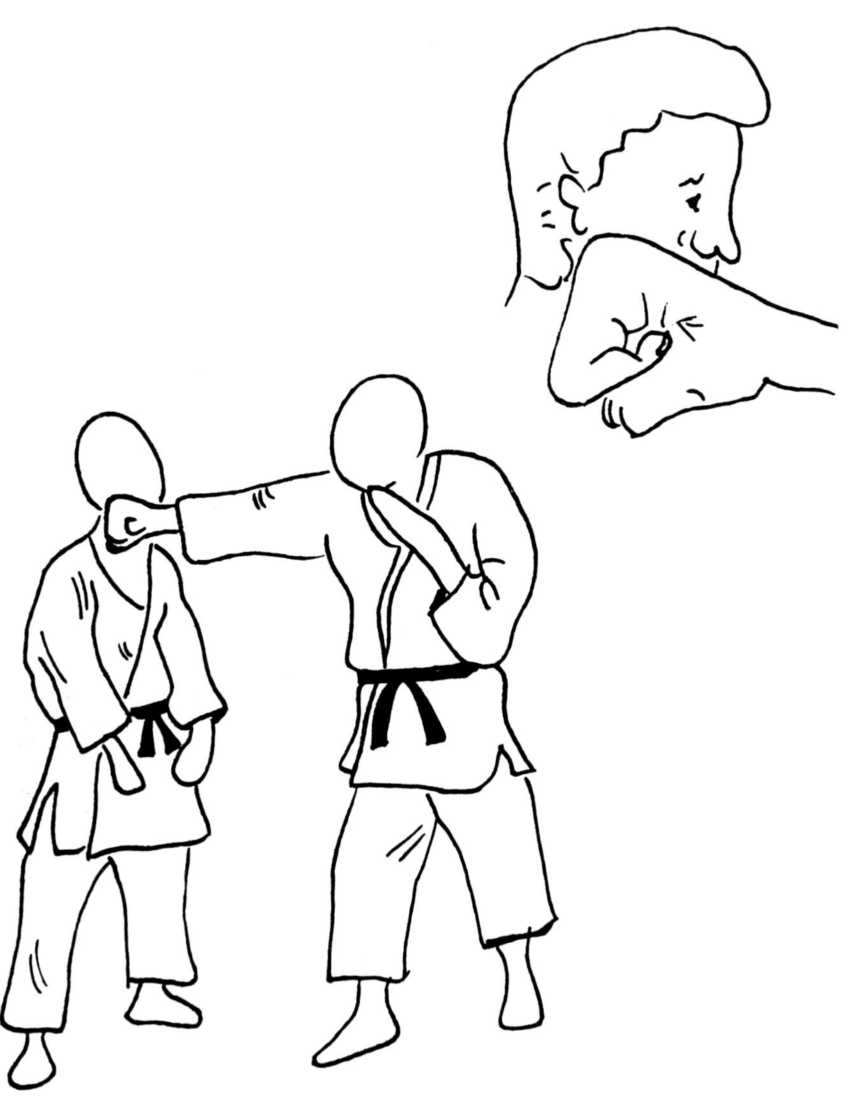

This technique is worthy of practice and can be extremely effective. The importance being to note the location of the strike, and practice on a punch bag to build focus with safety.

5 HAMMER FIST TO GROIN/BACK FIST TO FACE.

Here, the use of a quick double strike, shows how atemi moves the attacker, so as to maximise the effect without having to pull or shove a heavier attacker. Pain does the moving.

6 BACK FIST (RIKEN UCHI)to nose.

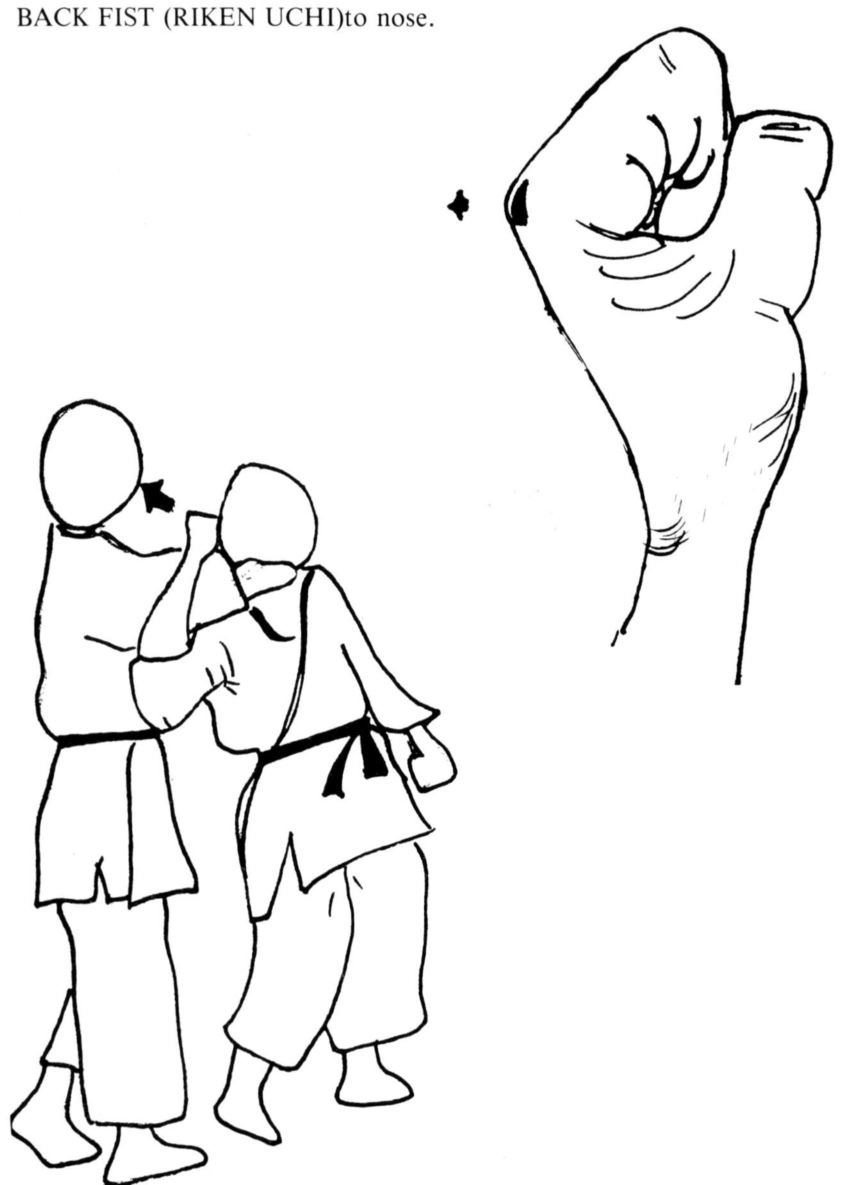

A very quick strike, which should be practiced on the pads or bag for focus and speed without over-extending the elbow. Note one's wrist should be flexible and like the movements of a birds wings. One's two main knuckles should strike, not the flat back of your hand. If it does it will hurt you and not have the desired effect on the attacker.

7 KNUCKLE STRIKE (HIRAKEN) to point under the nose.

Note the alignment of the fingers and how the force of the blow is amplified by being concentrated into a small area; a most versatile strike.

8 PALM HEEL (TEISHO-UCHI) to under the jaw.

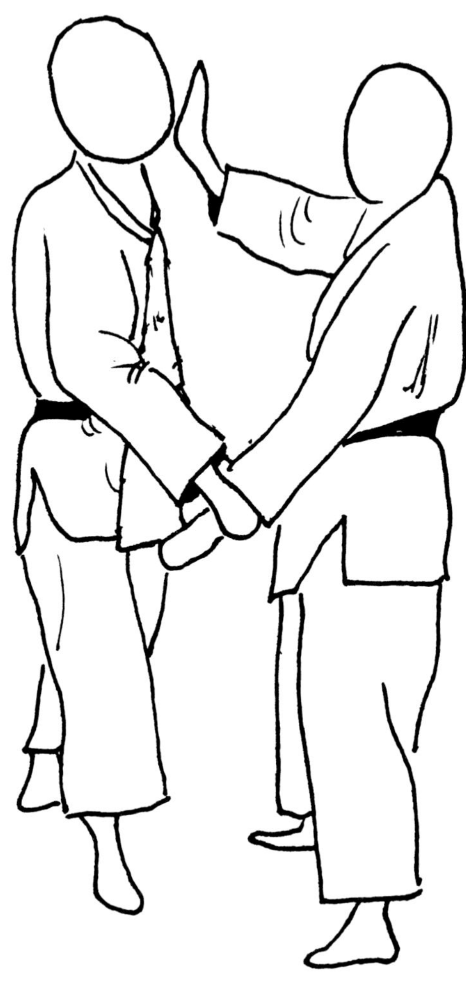

This is a corner stone technique of atemi, particularly suitable for ladies with long nails who have trouble forming a fist. It allows great force to be delivered even by the less experienced without the fear of damaging the hand that can be associated with punching by novices. Many would argue that an open hand is more deadly by virtue of its speed.

9 PALM HEEL (TEISHO-UCHI) to side of the jaw.

The crossing version of the palm heel strike allows the jaw to be easily dislocated and a lock perhaps applied as the attacker is subdued by the initial strike. This preliminary strike removes the need for strength in a potential grappling position.

10 KNEE (HIZA-UCHI) to the groin.

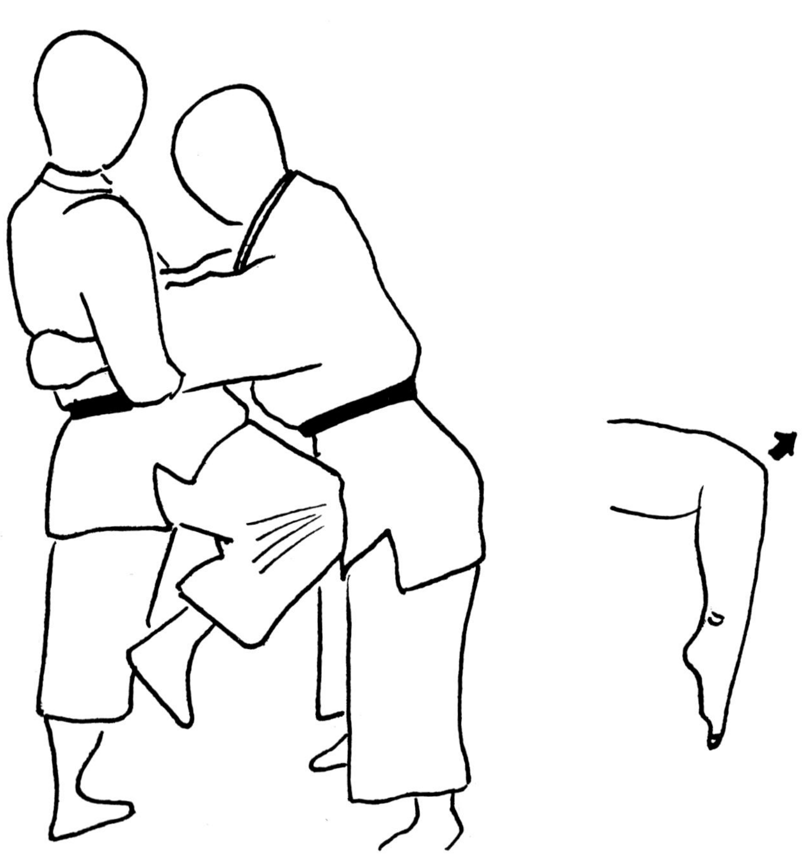

This is a simple and powerful technique, however note the position of the toes so as to present the correct boney surface of the knee and not as often done incorrectly, the flat of the thigh.

11 STAMP KICK (FUMIKOMI) to the foot.

Self explanatory but note that one should practise with a high knee lift movement so as to ensure enough lift of the knee when under pressure mentally. If you only move a little in practise, when it comes to using it for real, you may not have sufficient action in your movement to cause the pain you require to your adversary. Note that one can also run the shoe down the shin to cause pain and gain a release etc.

12 FRONT KICK (MAE-GERI)

Remember, do not kick full force without a target that you can actually make contact with, as you may damage your knee over a period of time. This technique requires balance, focus, flexibility and power, in achieving these speed will almost certainly follow after much practise.

13 ELBOW (EMPI-UCHI) back elbow.

A technique that is simple and yet very effective when in close to your assailant or if he is at close quarters behind you. By practising on a punch bag, you will ensure that you are striking with the point part of the elbow rather than the upper flat part diminishing the strikes effectiveness.

14 REVERSE RISING KNIFE HAND against breast grab.

The correct alignment of the bones in the hand is essential to prevent damage when striking with force. Practise forming the hand (with thumb tucked well in) and utilise a striking pad to condition your hand to generate great force without self injury.

15 SINGLE KNUCKLE (IPPONKEN) to gain release.

Perhaps this technique best illustrates how an atemi can also be a grappling technique. In the first application one can strike at the target, in the second a driving and rotating action will cause much the same effect.

16 PINCH (TSUKKAMI UCHI)

By pinching just near the femoral artery, a disproportionate amount of pain is generated without recourse to excessive permanent damage. A useful breakout technique and a valuable discourager of the over amorous person for the ladies to utilise.

ATEMI WAZA

Application of atemi against actual multiple assault.

From an interest point of view many schools of Ju-Jitsu place less emphasis on kicking than others. It should be noted, however, that whilst "each to their own", kicking was and still is an essential part of the gentle or pliable science.

Some typical kicks used in Ju-Jitsu.

N.B. In a real combat situation these kicks would generally be used to low point targets (below chest).

Practising to higher targets can increase flexibility and broaden one's knowledge of Ju-Jitsu atemi and other striking arts.

BACK KICK (USHIRO-GERI)

SIDE KICK (YOKO-GERI)

ROUNDHOUSE KICK (MAWASHI-GERI)

ROUNDHOUSE KICK. (using the shin).

CHAPTER FOUR

BLOCKING, EVADING AND TRAPPING

This area of Ju-Jitsu is a fascinating study, as many theories on blocking exist as do styles of martial arts.

One common theme is that of "not getting hit". In a real street situation one must be aware of the reality that your antagonist is likely to get some blows through onto your person. Your training should thus make you better able to avoid the 'big shots' likely to put you down but be prepared to feel the pain of being hit if you are in a real conflict situation, especially if against a forceful and hard attacker. Skill and practise minimise the likelihood of being struck but physiologically one must be prepared. Most Ju-Jitsu styles utilise the principle of body movement, that is keeping the force of an attack going and using this momentum to defeat the attacker. After all, the term 'pliable science' refers to this phenomena. However, when one is beginning ones studies or merely in the first stages of expertise, it may be advisable to utilise various simple blocking manoeuvres combined with an atemi strike or two to distract or anaesthetise the antagonist prior to locking, throwing etc. Knowing when and how to utilise an attackers force directly is a matter of practise and experience. The skill of blocking needs a great deal of explanation, physical and practical tuition. However, here are a few of the many blocking techniques which really deflect an attack from its target rather like a goal keeper does at football. The term blocking might better described the trapping or pre-emptive skills which we will look at shortly.

SHUTO UKE—KNIFE HAND BLOCK.

This is executed as if one was using the arm like a sword. The block executed with force can damage an antagonists attacking limb. Note, grabbing the blocked limb is a further common trait in Ju-Jitsu. This allows the attacker to be locked, thrown or made subject to a takedown.

SOTO-UDE-UKE—OUTSIDE FOREARM BLOCK.

The arm is used to deflect an oncoming blow to (a) the face; (b) the mid section and the defenders body is also pivoted out of the line of attack. Note, there are many further applications of the forearm as an instrument of blocking.

GEDAN-BARAI—LOWERING BLOCK.

Note the closed fist to avoid injury to the fingers or wrist of the defender. It is essential to strike immediately to prevent the incoming antagonist landing a fist strike.

KNEE AND SHIN BLOCK.

By using the front leg the quick attacks to low point targets can be blocked. NOTE: the position of the foot depends on the type of incoming kick being blocked.

It is important that the groin is shielded by the knee and shin thus allowing arms to continue protecting the upper torso.

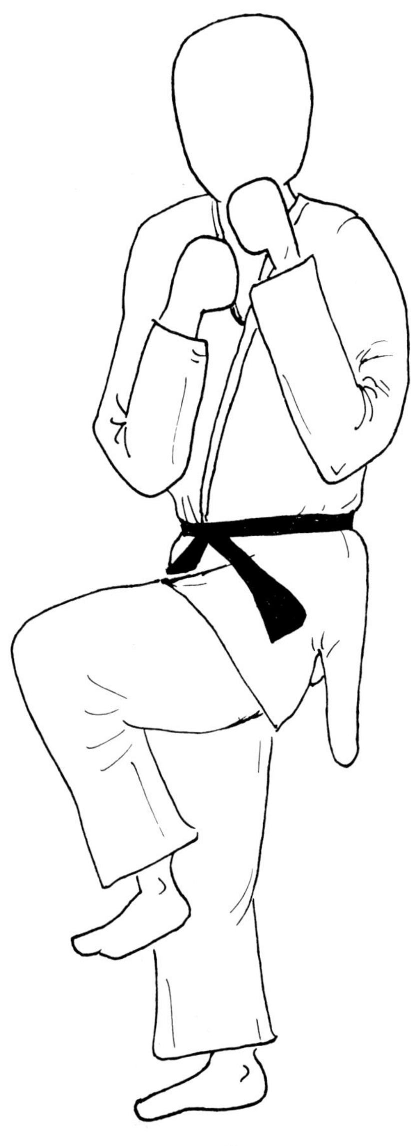

SUKUI-UKE—SCOOPING BLOCK.

A method of blocking which allows the defender to evade and throw an incoming kicker without recourse to great strength.

AGE-UKE—RISING BLOCK.

This block can be performed with a knife hand or closed fist. Some styles use an almost flat arm. The more appropriate method today because of long sleeves is the closed fist and a slanting arm finishing position. Try an experiment; get an individual to push at your shoulders or chest (slowly and in appropriate stance, having regard to safety). If you then block the pushing arm with a rising block and ask him/her to push, the force of the push will dissipate as your arm directs the force up and away, like the roof of a house causing the rain to run off rather than gathering and the weight of the collected water causing the roof to collapse.

B pushes A back.

The force is deflected if a corectly used rising block is affected. If B does continue to push, they place themselves in an ideal position for A to utilise atemi. To substantiate the angle of the arm recommended, remember how it was the snow causing the willow bow to bend and thus the snow to fall off which survived whilst the seemingly sturdier trees snapped under the weight of the collected snow.

This example from nature was the inspiration of the founder of Honti Yoshin Ryu-(Willow Hearted School).

TEISHO—UKE—PALM HEEL BLOCK.

A very simple blocking method where the palm is utilised like a strike to re-direct or neutralise a blow.

NOTE, this list is far from comprehensive; it is only an attempt to show some of the basic blocking methods utilised in the vast area of martial skills called Ju-Jitsu, formerly Yawara Jutsu.

Evasion is the simplest to define but harder to master as a skill (not being where the aimed assault strikes or cuts (in the case of bladed weapons)). Patterns of movement can be learnt from both armed and unarmed disciplines. The sword, for example, utilises extensively the removal of ones body from the line of attack. The Japanese sword with its wonderful edge placed less emphasis on blocking than in the western rapier sword play sense. Thus, much of Ken Jutsu special strategy has relevance in the use of unarmed and armed Ju-Jitsu skills.

Trapping is a means of stemming an attack by trapping the likely offending limb as can be seen in the photographs.

NOTE, how in the case of the lock, Tori is trapping Ukes leg which otherwise might strike to Toris groin.

CHAPTER FIVE

THE ART OF BREAKFALLING

This is a much neglected part of Ju-Jitsu in many schools. The reason being that it hurts a great deal when you start and requires regular practise to maintain it at a good level.

The art of breakfalling can be described as the science of learning how to take a fall without sustaining shock or injury. The term "breakfall" comes from the action of striking the ground just prior to the main part of the body hitting the ground. This acts as a shock absorber and also balances the body to prevent the recoil from jerking the head back and allowing hard contact with the floor which would otherwise cause injury.

There are some very useful philosophical lessons to be learnt from breakfalling. Dr Kano used to say that it was a lesson for life, one should meet troubles with all your being rather than trying to prevent the inevitable. In breakfalling, an untrained person may put out an arm to try and prevent the fall. By so doing, they often break a collar bone or wrist. The trained individual will relax into the fall meeting the adversity with all his person (using a breakfalling technique) and thus be able to jump up unscathed.

On a more humorous note, I have heard breakfalling described as 'the art of hurling oneself in the air, making as much noise as is possible on landing and then getting up pretending it did not hurt'. Those who have tried to run before they can walk in breakfalling terms will see the humour and the 'sting in the tail' of this little humorous description.

In serious terms, like most physical actions, a series of pictures will best show the execution of the most commonly used breakfalls (see sequences as shown). It must be remembered that when one is beginning, floor drills, where the fall is practised with little or no take off is the best policy. This allows the students confidence to grow and the body to adapt and strengthen. To perform breakfalls from too low a position once the basic landing positions have been mastered is also folly. If one is trying to block attacks and practise against slow ones, one will be unable to deal with a very speedy attack. With body conditioning one must start gently at first, but with knockdown or full contact (such as a boxer experiences) one does eventually have to enter a vigorous training regime prior to contest. Likewise with falls, in the street there are no mats thus in the Yawara Ryu schools under my present tuition, potential black belts have to breakfall with good height on a wooden floor and then on a concrete surface. If you have always executed breakfalls gently or from a low starting position, flaws in your technique will never be discovered. The switch to a hard non-matted floor soon shows the little unseen faults in ones technique which can cause those nasty cuts and even chipped or broken bones. Thus it is from a realistic point of view rather than an aesthetic standpoint that at the blackbelt and high kyu grade stage breakfalls should be effected from a reasonably high starting position. To those longer in the tooth, the height should be appropriate to their age and condition. Certainly older men and women who engage in activities such as Ju-Jitsu and Judo where breakfalling is a regular part of their practise, tend to be less susceptable to broken bones than their non-training peers. This can be accounted for on two accounts; firstly, bone is maleable over a period of time, that is the skeleton can be affected by ones activities for better or for worse; secondly, the trained person is likely to be in a better state of health generally than his more lethargic peers. Also, the skills acquired in youth can be maintained at a certain level even into old age, as many great masters of the martial arts demonstrate admirably. A further story of interest concerns a conversation that I once had with a karate expert who had only a limited knowledge of the art of breakfalling. He was challenging the relevance of this section of Goshin Jutsu (modern self defence or Jutsu). I explained that one may be grounded at speed, and from a ladies' or gentlemen's self defence standpoint if one broke an arm, collar bone, wrist, etc. in the fall, all the good tuition in an upright standing position would be of little use. I can also recount two cases of people who I have taught using their breakfalling skills to save their lives, and can personally vouch for the substance of these events. Firstly, a coal miner found his forward roll got him out of the way of a piece of machinery that was falling from a hoist. The piece of machinery weighed several tons and he described that without the instinctive movement that he had learnt in his training he would have definitely been killed or crippled. The second example occurred when one of my most senior students, Sensei Robert Marshall, a farmer by profession, fell off a roof. He landed in a side breakfall position and whilst badly bruised, shaken and experiencing localised cuts, walked away to tell the tale. In his own words, "If I did not know how to breakfall I could well be in a wheelchair or have at least fractured my skull from the shock waves travelling up my legs and spine to my skull." The farmhouse was a two storey building and although by grasping at the water pipes he slowed his fall, the 'proof of the pudding' lies in the fact that one week later he was back at training.

Looking at the following breakfalls you will see differences, all be it minor ones, compared with the more usually advocated Judo type falls. Remember that Judo has developed towards the road of an Olympic sport, also primarily the falls are designed to work on a mat.

The Ju-Jitsu fall must bear the likely consequences of falling on a hard surface although for safety and comforts sake a greater part of the practise is either on a matted area or sprung floor. For example, if one slaps the concrete as in a side breakfall with a perfectly flat hand, you will see it turn the colour of a beetroot and feel it throb with pain. The action on concrete is modified slightly so that the palm heel area is used to hit the ground and prevent the aforementioned phenomena.

Below are a range of sequential photographs showing the advanced application of several breakfalls. After this I have shown the most commonly used falls illustrating the practise or beginners' method. (NOTE, don't try to run before you can walk.) For the experienced person, please note that there are many variations and that the only valid ones are those that work when done from a good height and have regard to strategic factors like countering and defending against an attacker. However, for ease of analysis it must be stated that these are some of the more effective when performed on a very hard or hostile surface.

SIDE BREAKFALL

One side shown, reverse for other side.

NOTE how the ankles are kept off the floor preventing injury to them and also this allows better protection against attacks to the groin.

FRONT FALL

On this breakfall it is important to keep the toes curled well back thus enabling a safe landing and quick counter attack.

Allow the body to be like a spring and ensure that the flat of the forearms and palm heels slap the floor (this does sting on a hard surface but the important thing is that you are not damaged and able therefore to execute counter techniques if required).

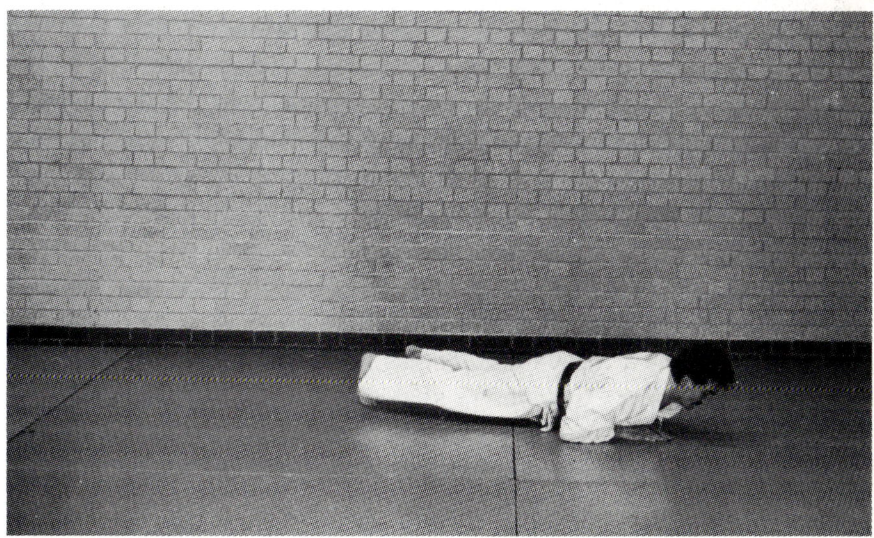

BACKWARD FALL

Too often even senior grades practise this from a rolling posture. Thus, real situational use of this breakfall is missed.

NOTE that the head must be well tucked in and use the arms strongly.

FLIP OVER
An advanced test of landing position and special awareness.

HANDSTAND BREAKFALL

It is important to do this fall on the move ensuring that the arms are straight having made contact with the floor, quickly moving to the sides of the student once the legs and body have moved through the highest point of the handstand.

FORWARD ROLL

NOTE how the lead right arm is swung through pushing off the right leg. The roll is an oblique forward roll, not a gymnastic forward roll (weight should travel over the scapulas).

FORWARD ROLLS over objects

NOTE the way in which the scapulas take the main weight. This movement was called an oblique forward roll by S. K. Uyenishi.

HANDS & KNEES

RANDOM BREAKFALLS ON CONCRETE

BACKWARD ROLL

The primary object is to keep the head clear of the floor and to roll over in an oblique fashion.

NB. It is not a gymnastics back roll and legs must be synchronised with the arms.

Finish into appropriate stance facing antagonist demonstrating zanshin (awareness)

BREAKFALLS FOR BEGINNERS

SIDE BREAKFALL

FRONT BREAKFALL

CHAPTER SIX

THROWING TECHNIQUES

Historically, it is claimed that Dr. Kano took the mechanically most efficient throws from Ju-Jitsu and produced his eclectic system of Jui do. It must be remembered that throwing was a part of Ju-Jitsu but only one of the component parts. Many of the throws used in Ju-Jitsu relied on painful locks to ensure that the antagonist could not escape or counter. Judo itself changed as Olympic sport recognition has lead to major reforms. Many techniques have been removed as sporting considerations take precedence over self-defence or martial arts criteria.

The idea that Dr. Kano saw Judo as replacing traditional arts is a false one. As an educationalist he wanted a format suitable for use in schools as a form of physical culture, a training for life. He wanted to preserve much of the ancient arts which were in popular decline as their harsh training methods and painful techniques had a limited mass appeal. As for throwing contests, one must remember that many Ju-Jitsu schools placed greater emphasis on their atemi than their throwing. Certainly the use of surprise and painful locks, holds or pre throw atemi strikes made the potentially less mechanically correct throwing methods of many Ju-Jitsu schools extremely practical and effective when done for real. One identifiable weakness of some of the older schools of Ju-Jitsu was that their systems had become over ritualised and revolved heavily around the practise of forms to the detriment of free practise for safety reasons. This is not a criticism of formalised training, but once human life was recognised as sacred much of the evolution through trial that had made Ju-Jitsu so much an effective art suddenly disappeared. Having said this, many schools famed for their harsh training have successfully kept alive the spirit and techniques of Ju-Jitsu and this spirit is well and alive today not only in Japan but also world-wide.

BALANCE AND THROWING

If one uses a chair, one can easily see how by pulling or pushing in the classically named eight directions of balance one can easily topple the chair.

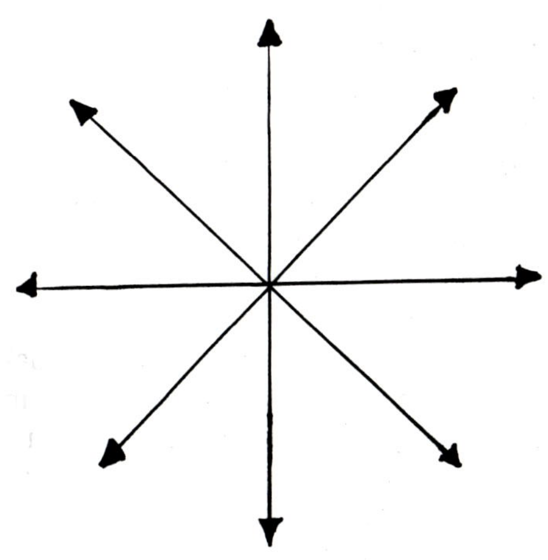

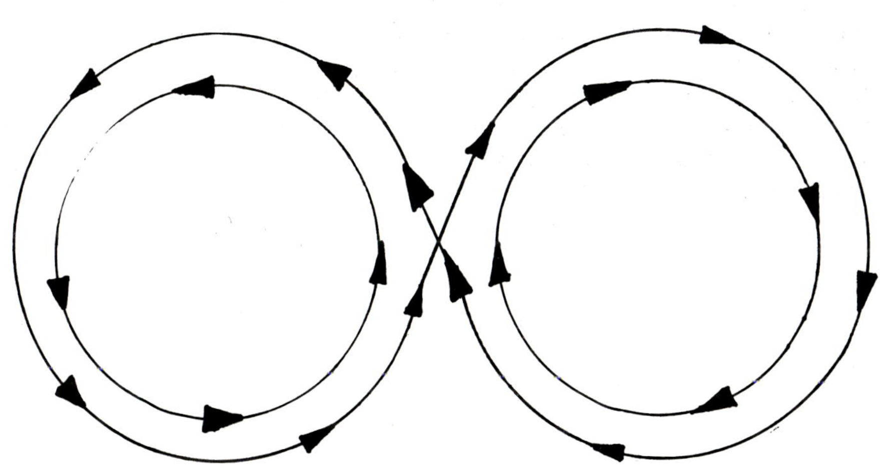

THROWING FROM A PUSH
(For appropriate finishes see stomach throw, later in text).

NOTE how tori keeps attackers force going rather than trying to meet force with force.

THROWING FROM A PULL

NOTE how tori when pulled steps to the diagonal and breaks ukes balance to the rear diagonal facilitating ease of throw.

THROWING FROM A MAN CIRCLING

INNER THICH THROW

From these basic eight directions and by way of infinite methods of pushing, pulling, lifting, downwards pressure etc., even the heaviest person can be unbalanced if ones skill is sufficiently greater than the other persons.

In Ju-Jitsu the use of the attackers momentum or force is utilised to enhance their downfall. Body movement is used not only by re-directing an attackers force but by way of body turns. Tai Sabbaki is shown in many Ju-Jitsu movements and Aikido has attempted to further develop this skill. (See illustration on circular movement p.67.) "If one is pushed-pull; if one is pulled-push", a simple theme taken a stage further by Mifune Sensei who said in his

'Cannons of Judo', "If pushed, circle back; if pulled, step to the diagonal". This is useful advice if one is engaged in a throwing contest.

Throws can be classified in many ways, however one school of thought says that there are only five throws and infinite variations of performing such throws. Other schools of thought would contest this, however for ease of writing, let us utilise the simplistic analysis and say that throws may be classified under five headings for convenience:
Hand throws;
Leg throws;
Shoulder throws;
Hip throws;
Sacrifice throws.

If one takes many styles of Ju-Jitsu with their multiple variations combined with take downs etc., the number of identifiable techniques of a single school may run into the hundreds. However, as a wide based introduction to Ju-Jitsu, we will look at two of each type being used in self defence, countering against actual common assaults.

HAND THROWS

WRIST WHEEL against a straight thrust to mid section.

Having thrown the attacker a wrist lock is used to hold him; atemi could be applied if necessary.

HEAD TWIST against a front choke.
(SAFETY NOTE: only use this technique in a real situation as it can cause irreparable damage to the ears, when practising this throw only do it slowly and gently).

The defender applies a double cupped palm strike to attackers ears. If used for real (full force) finish would be optional as attacker would be severely disorientated. (Use lock of atemi as appropriate.)

HOCK against a straight punch.
Defender uses a knife hand block, also stepping out of the line of attack and delivers a palm heel.

Defender then uses a HOCK throw; this is like a reap except that theheel of the throwing leg strikes a vulnerable point on the attackers calf rendering his lower leg temporarily immobilised, (note for safety practise calf to calf) stamp kick used to finish. (NOTE: care must be exercised when practising stamp kicks).

LEG SWEEP

NOTE how the defender uses atemi strike to unbalance the attacker as well as grasping and pulling the attacking limb prior to the throw with the sweep. The sweeping action must be generated from the hips as well as the leg as using the leg alone will be insufficient.

LEG REAP

SHOULDER THROWS

SHOULDER DROP against a bar strangle from the rear.
Defender uses back elbow to loosen and weaken attack
Defender throws attacker
NOTE how this throw brings attackers weight slightly around the side of toris body (feeling of stealing the attackers space when throwing)
Finish with appropriate atemi or lock.
N.B. Always finish antagonist once you have thrown him.
From a technical point of view the Japanese word for shoulder throws often uses Seio- which actually means 'to carry on the back'.

HALF SHOULDER THROW against a hooking blow.
Attack and block;
Defender uses an advancing elbow strike to sternum;
Defender positions himself @ 90° to attacker and executes arm break;
(NOTE if one does not trap the arm correctly as shown the break will often fail).

Throw
(NOTE how the pain of a broken or dislocated arm aids the defender in completing his technique).

Some incorrectly think that shoulder throws only require a pulling motion as if clearing a sack of coal from ones back. It must be remembered that just like a labourer or coalman, one must use your legs to place the antagonist in the correct position prior to pulling, twisting and unloading ones adversary to the floor.

WINDING THROW

Another variation of shoulder throw utilising elbow atemi.
NOTE finish with arm break and double knee pin.

HIP THROW against a hooking blow.

Defender uses a knife hand block and punch to solar plexis; Grasping firmly round the head, waist or under arm of attacker, the defender can either ensure chest contact remembering to keep his head low and affect a major hip throw or else force his loin well across in front of the attacker and thus affect a loin wheel hip throw;

Finish with descending hammer fist followed by back fist to groin and locking with goose neck lock (wrist crush lock).

NOTE how the knees are used to pin the attacker and prevent any counter attack.

Multiple atemi ensure that the attacker can not ki up as speed of blows would defy almost any exponent transfering his ki focus at equal speed to the blows.

SPRING HIP THROW against a right cross (boxing style).

Defender executes a knife hand and inside forearm block, following immediately with hammer fist to the attackers head. This puts attacker slightly back and in a fairly upright position.

Having grasped hold of the attackers jacket and arm with the knife hand blocking hand and putting the other hand so as to grasp plenty of hair (ear if the attacker is bald), defender lifts attacker on to his toes.

Defender steps in, as shown in photo sequence and uses the side of his bent leg to make contact with the attackers forward leg.

Defender also allows his hip to make contact with attackers groin and by driving through the attackers position the defender is able to affect a very high fast throw on the almost false spring like hip that his bent leg has created.

Finish with reverse step over arm lock.

CRAB CLAW SCISSORS

NOTE how tori (defender) utilises his arm on the floor to support himself whilst affecting scissor movement within his legs.

Finish with descending heel atemi.

STOMACH THROW

This is a useful way of throwing someone whose force is coming directly at you with speed or slower but forcibly.

Attack is a pushing double lapel seizure.

Defender places his foot in the attackers stomach but note in a suitable position and with knee slightly bent.

Defender, like the hub of a wheel, sits down as close to the attackers feet as possible.

Defender affects the throw using his arms to prevent the attacker from collapsing on him. By straightening his leg at the right moment and encouraging the attackers forward motion, a hard fall can be affected. Tori throws uke into the wall.

Alternative finish; tori keeps hold of ukes lapel, quickly spinning around executing a strangle whilst covering eyes against ukes counter attack.

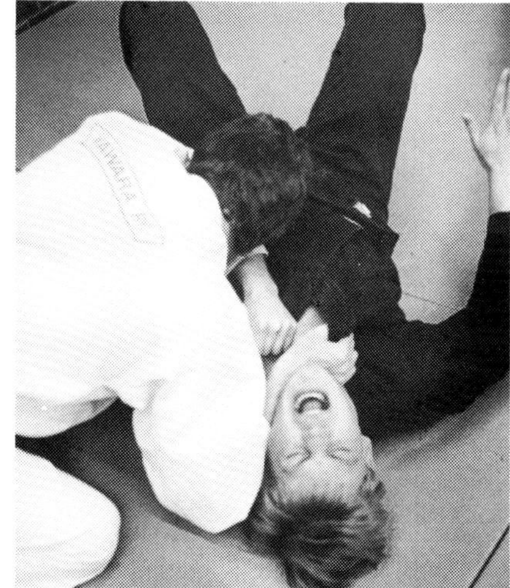

LATERAL SEPARATION THROW

In ancient times when loin cloths were worn this throw would be effected not by the belt but by the testicles. The name thus becomes self explanatory.

Attack is a lunge punch to the head.
Evasion followed by the throw;
Finish with kick to the head.

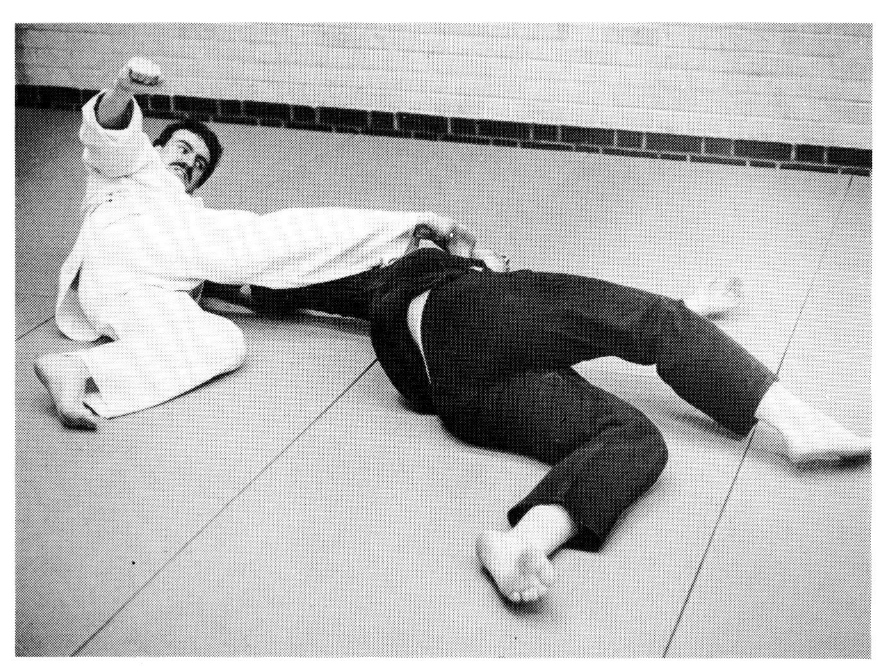

CHAPTER SEVEN

KATAME WAZA

This section of Ju-Jitsu is perhaps the most intricate of all the sciences sections. It covers the locking of joints, the application of neck locks and strangles and the martial skill of wrenching. Many other miscellaneous skills connected with grappling would also fit into this area of study such as flesh tearing, biting and eviction techniques as well crushing, choking and suffocating and many others too numerous to mention and list here.

For the average student of Ju-Jitsu, the skills most relevant to him would be those of locking the fingers, wrist, arm, neck and legs. Diato Ryu Aiki Ju-Jitsu gave great emphasis to locking the wrist; the founders of Hapkido were greatly influenced by this school's emphasis. Without any doubt, the foremost world recognised exponent of wrist locks is Professor Wally Jay 10th Dan. I have been privileged to both feel and discuss his small circle theory of locking which places great influence on the use of the defender's wrist in application of techniques. It also utilises a vast number of wrist locks and combined throwing methods.

Finger locks are useful in the self defence and breakout areas of Ju-Jitsu. The ancient Greeks and Roman pugalists made every effort to break their opponents small joints when contesting. The size of these joints allows a weaker adversary to gain advantage without having to combat greater strength which is so much more amplified in the larger limbs, for example arms, legs.

FINGER LOCK, against an assault in the car.
NOTE the way that the defender controls the attacker forcing him to stop the car. More drastic tactics might cause both to be injured or killed if the car were to crash, this also illustrates the potential folly of these so called experts who always advocate the maximum damage tactics in all situations.

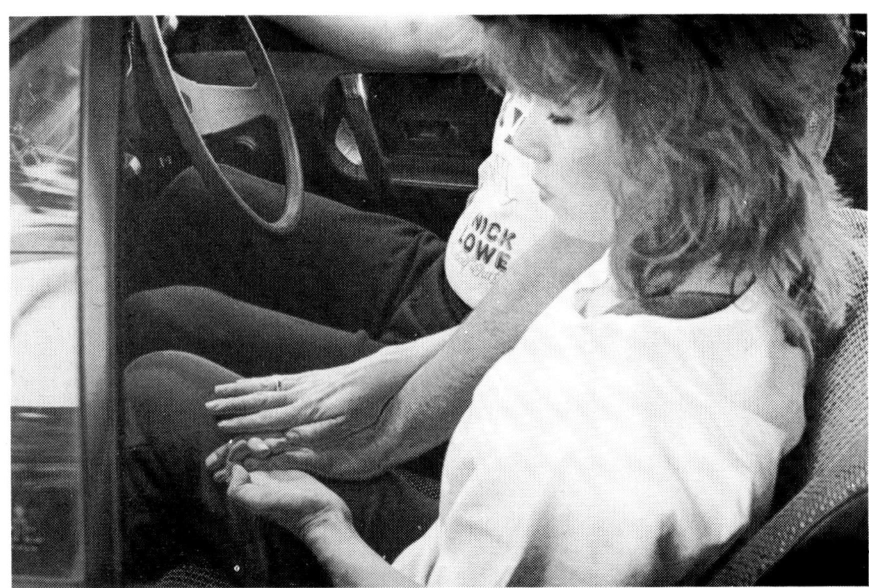

NB in reality hand is anchored down by other hand as in photo 1.

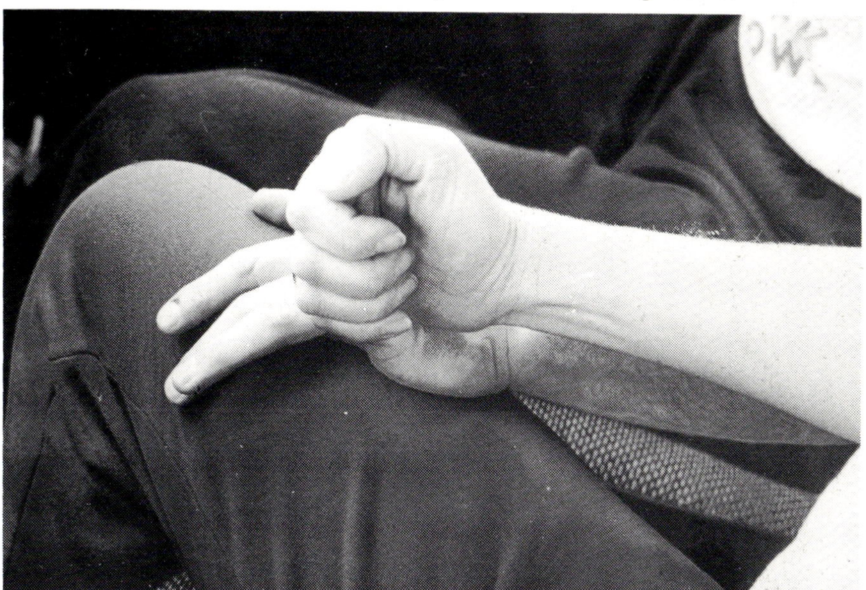

Application of same finger lock as an eviction technique.

NOTE the defender block strikes with the palm heel and by swiftly applying a goose neck wrist lock he can take down or evict antagonist dependant on the antagonist's condition after the atemi strike and overall circumstances.

WRIST LOCK against lapel seizure.

Defender grasps the attacking limb at the wrist, delivers a kick to the shin as a pre-release, applying downward and outward pressure on the attacker's wrist and elbow causing his arm to bend. With a twist of the attacker's wrist, an excruciatingly painful wrist lock is effected.

FINISH: Knee kick to head.

LADIES SELF DEFENCE APPLICATION (arm around the waist).
NOTE position of the defender's thumb to effect the lock.

ARM PIN
Applying pressure on the elbow joint, wrist and shoulder.

STEP OVER STANDING.
Ensure a gentle stamp kick (in practise). In a real situation the jaw would dislocate or break preventing the attacker biting ones Achilles tendon.

NOTE. Step over arm lock can also be used as a reclining version.

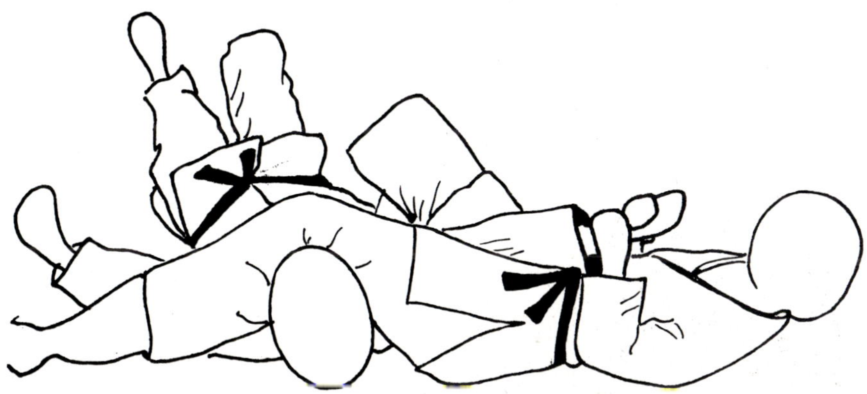

RECLINING VERSION
NB. Ensure that ukes jaw is dislocated by atemi or kick to prevent him biting as a counter.

TWO ARM LOCKS (use of whilst ground fighting).
Tori uses his legs to lock ukes arm; tori is also controlling ukes other arm and head with his hands.
NB. To effect this lock using the legs, considerable repetitive practise is necessary, however, once mastered this is a combat effective move in conjunction with atemi such as head butt.

ARM BREAK utilised against a rear choke.
Defender escapes by utilising pressure against attacker's thumb with the back of his neck.

Having broken the limb, a throw may easily be effected or a take down.

ACHILLES TENDON LOCK (standing version)

NOTE how the ankle crush lock immobilises the antagonist and allows the lock to have full effect.

It is important to ensure that pressure is exerted, in sporting contests, with the defender's heel in the stomach of the attacker's but in self defence the groin gives great advantage.

LEG LOCK

Defender evades attacker's punch and by quickly and adeptly inserting his legs, as shown in the photographs, he effects a most painful and useful leg lock and take down.

NOTE carefully the exact position of the legs and knees or else you will fail to fully lock the attacker.

LEG LOCK

This can be better described as an ankle lock.

NOTE the way the use of both of the defender's arms face the joint in the exact reverse position of the joints normal flex. This technique can be utilised if one is grappling on the floor.

NECK LOCKS

DO NOT PRACTISE WITHOUT TRAINED PERSON IN REVIVAL TECHNIQUES PRESENT.

NAKED STRANGLE
NOTE that in a self-defence situation one must bury ones eyes as shown or else the attacker may respond by gouging your eyes.

ENTWINING NAKED STRANGLE
NOTE that one must bury ones eyes and to practise on both sides to gain proficiency.

THRUSTING CHOKE
As can be seen in the photograph, a push full force is exerted against the neck and wind pipe. Bury the eyes when using in actual fighting in the street self-defence situation. (NOTE this had not been done in the photo in order to illustrate the position of hands.)

A CHOKE

EAGLES CLAW
The picture is self explanatory but a degree of caution must be used when practising this technique. Whilst certain exponents can use ki or are very physically strong and can use this to resist this technique, its effects are quite dramatic and damage may result if it is used forcibly.
NOTE that one actully attempts to rip the wind pipe out if the circumstances such as preserving life so require.

CRUSHING

KNEE CRUSH TO THE CHEST

NOTE the use of the jacket to gain a pulling force and the exact position of the knee on the sternum. This technique is more applicable to ground contesting.

NB. Do not use in training on persons with any heart condition, however mild.

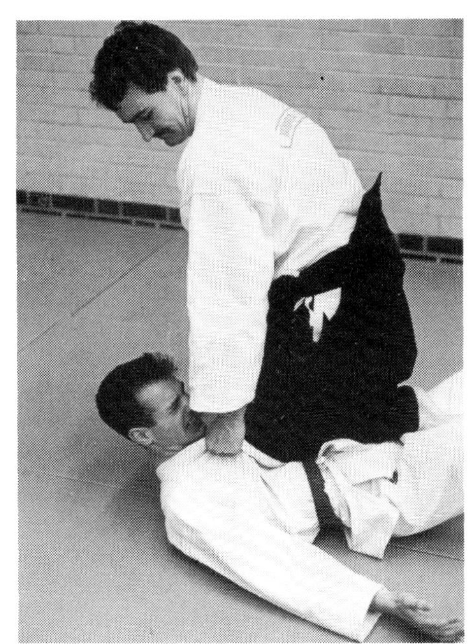

RANDOM COUNTERS TO ASSAULTS

FRONT STRANGLE utilising FINGER to STERNUM CLAVICLE NOTCH

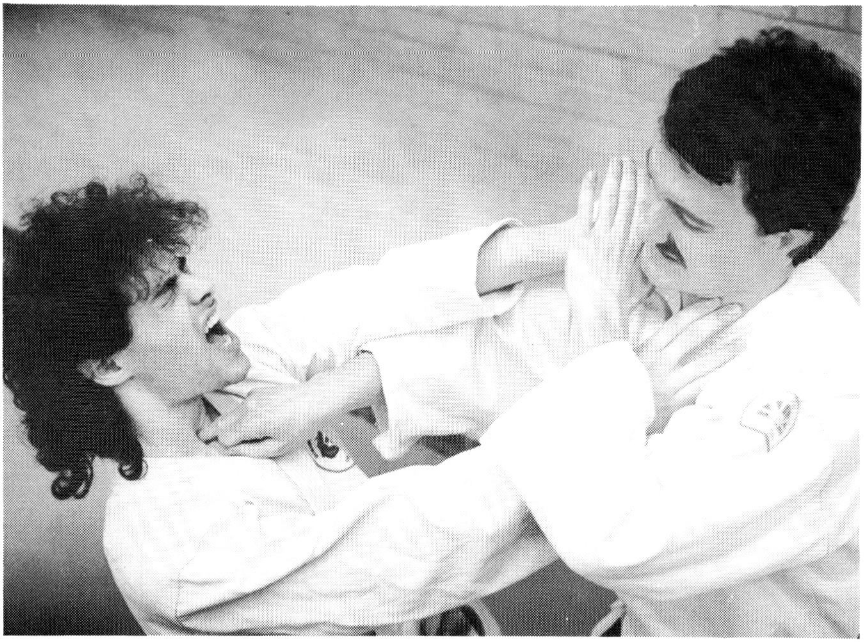

HEAD CHANCERY

DEFENCE TO REAR BAR STRANGLE

Where throw not appropriate.
NB. Alternative use of arm pin.

CHAPTER EIGHT

GROUND FIGHTING

This is a topic where a degree of specialist expertise can save your life. If you do end up being thrown to the ground the need to defend yourself is the primary aim. Certain principles can be applied but it must be remembered that this is a topic worthy of many years of study. The subject can be broken up into several areas:

(a) Defence against standing attacks;
(b) Techniques and tactics when both protagonists are on the floor;
(c) The competitive or free practise area of activity.

Defence to a kick.

Defence against a stamp kick.

NOTE: never attempt to catch the attacking foot; either roll away from the limb or towards the support leg.

There are many more such tactics and techniques but this would go beyond the scope of a book this size.

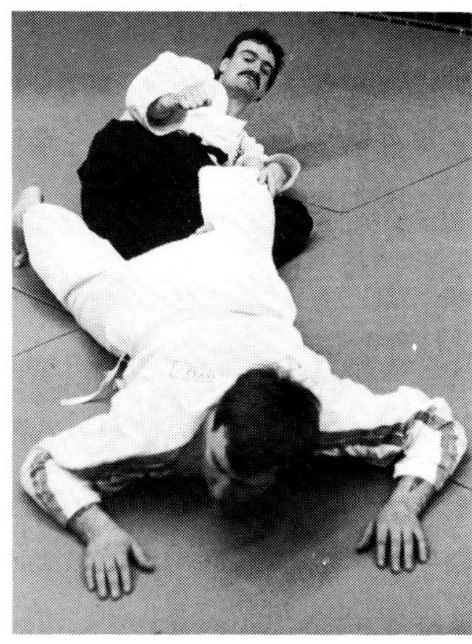

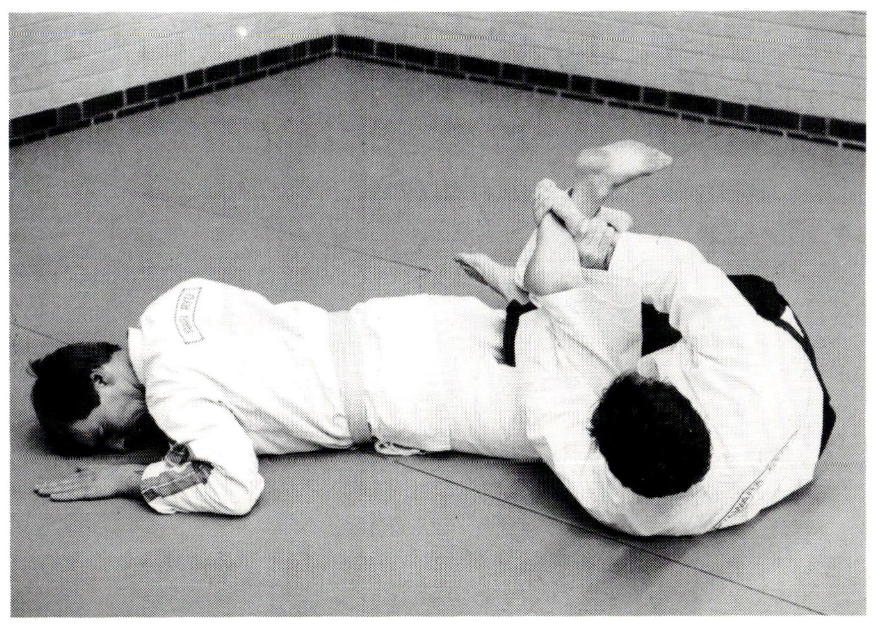

GRAPPLING IN GROUND WORK

The next main aspect of ground work relates to grappling on the floor. If one's life is at stake then the use of eye strikes and groin grabs (grab twist and pull) are obviously necessary. However, by mastering simple locks (already mentioned) in conjunction with three simple basic rules, good effect can be made of manœuvres in less drastic circumstances:

(1) Grab hold tightly but let go lightly.
(This means that if you have a hold or strangle on then go for it, but do not waste energy struggling over a grip or failing hold.

(2) Use the legs to move your antagonist away from you and deprive him of a good position.

(3) When moving, move fast but try to be relaxed and loose, excessive force or muscular tightness will only inhibit your movement. If what he is doing has no effect then don't struggle for no reason (remember, you are not subject to hold down scores as you would be in judo).

With regards to further exposition on this topic, I hope to produce a series of books dealing with each of the main aspects of Ju-Jitsu in the future.

For now, my advice is to learn the basic locks, strangles, chokes, etc. well; quality not quantity is the answer and if there are two moves generally the simplest will be the most effective.

To whet your appetite:
I have included here one ground fighting manœuvre which shows the use of legs and the skill of Katame Waza to good effect:
Reverse step over arm lock against strangle from between the legs.
(Use in self defence.)

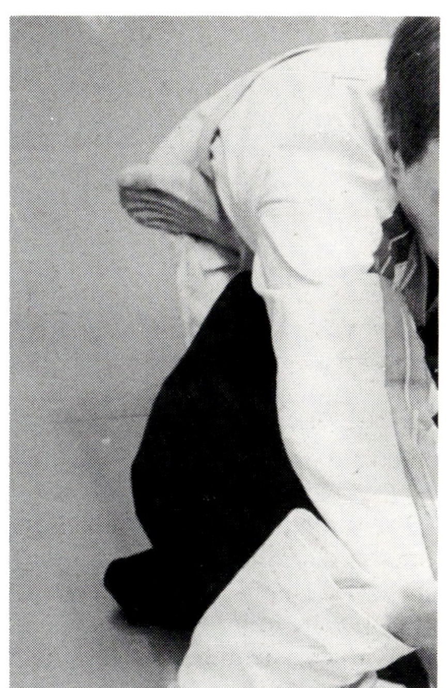

CHAPTER NINE

WEAPONRY

Referring back to the historical origins of Ju-Jitsu one can see that depending on your view or chosen analysis one can say Ju-Jitsu derived from weapons systems or that its roots lay in the latter unarmed sciences with their origins stemming from other Asian countries.

I prefer the analysis of the Victorian students of Ju-Jitsu who were after all training with men like Ranku Uyenishi's father who was actually a samurai. For me, information that is directly passed by oral tradition may historically be less fashionable but it does nevertheless have the benefit of being believed and passed on by men with direct links with the samurai. Even the formalised schools of Ju-Jitsu which sprang up in the relatively peaceful Edo period some regard to weaponry and the art of ancient weapons (Kobu-Jutsu) and Ju-Jitsu have many links.

The reason why the links become weaker is that much of the spread of Ju-Jitsu went hand in hand with Judo. By virtue of its aims with regards to physical culture and suitability for educational purposes, many of the more esoteric facets of the parent art Ju-Jitsu were excluded from general usuage (although seniors continued their practise at the Kodokan (also at the Budokwai in Great Britain) in the specialist studies that Dr. Kano required certain persons to undertake, like Professor Tominiki under Usheba).

The weapons associated with different schools or ryu depended greatly on the schools origin and history. Warriors who made friends would swap and share skills and thus schools weapons knowledge would often grow as new expertise was added. Thus today, some traditional schools have added the weapons that might be thought of as being Okinowan such as sai, tonfa, nunchuku, kama, 5′ and 6′ bo. These are not the traditional core weapons but by virtue of interchange they have come to be studied in some Japanese ryu.

The traditional weapons of the Ju-Jitsu school could consist of any of a long list plus any specialist studies particular to a school or ryu, however the most common being:

Roku-Shaku-Bo;	Manriki-Kusari; (weighted chain)
Han-Bo;	Katana; (sword)
Tanto;	Wakijashi;

Jo;	Naginata;
Ku-Bo; (Yawara stick)	Shiriken;
Nawa; (rope)	Shaiken;
Tessen; (iron fan)	Musari-gama; (sickle and chain)
Cane;	Chigiriki; (flail)

The most commonly practised however would be the stick weapons as these were both practical and realistic after the edict forbidding the wearing of swords.

Traditionally, weaponry being a very dangerous art with its potential for serious injury was practised in a tried and tested manner. Students learnt etiquette and discipline and began by learning Kihon i.e., basics.

These basics were normally practised by way of pre-learnt sequences. Thus a kihon sequence might have 8, 10 or 12 attacks which conformed to the lines of Happo Geri, whilst the sequence would also (working in pairs to get the feel of the real weapon) have blocks and counters. By constant practise the students learnt the basic movements which usually had hidden in this kihon sequence greater and more subtle uses.

Often students would then go on to learn prepared fight sequences which allowed a degree of realism and spacial movement to be absorbed. From here either further more advanced kata were learnt or further study revolved around the application of the techniques from that already assimilated.

Schools would go on to teach the use of grappling tactics to be employed both with and without the weapons.

The importance of weaponry can be emphasised by the following truths.

How can one learn to defend against an attack when one knows nothing of the type of an attack a weapon is capable of?

Do those practitioners who reckon on their ability to defend against an armed attack know of the skill that many weapons exponents possess?

I think that if they did they would be more aware of the difficulty of say disarming a swordsman or a trained knife attacker/fighter as opposed to the untrained hooligan or mugger.

Whilst on the subject of weaponry, my own school Yawara Ryu insists on its black belts attending basic annual firearms courses 'as ignorance can kill! If one knows about any weapon one is better qualified in its uses and also the potential to disarm someone wealding it. Knowing when not to act or when to be still is as important as knowing when to go for it.

Training smart is more important than just training hard. Traditional schools recognised this fact and that is why the teaching licences were awarded so as to differentiate between someone purely skilled in the art and the person able, willing and capable of transmitting the science to others.

The combined use of weapon and grappling skills was also taught but as a distinct study. Thus one learnt to throw shiriken and separately within the same school went on to learn how to utilise them like a knife and yawara stick.

Just like Japanese calligraphy has only 8 lines or strokes, so the classic cuts of the sword are defined within these 8 lines of attack. Thus it seems a very simple analysis, a kihon working within these 8 lines of attack; yet there are in both weaponry and calligraphy infinite variations. One must not be fooled by the simplicity of the sword Happo Geri or the Han-Bo various kihon sequences, their simplicity hides a lifetime study of information waiting for the student with enough stamina, spirit and wisdom to unlock the information contained within.

HAPPO GERI. Most Japanese weapons base their attacks on these eight classical lines or cut directions.

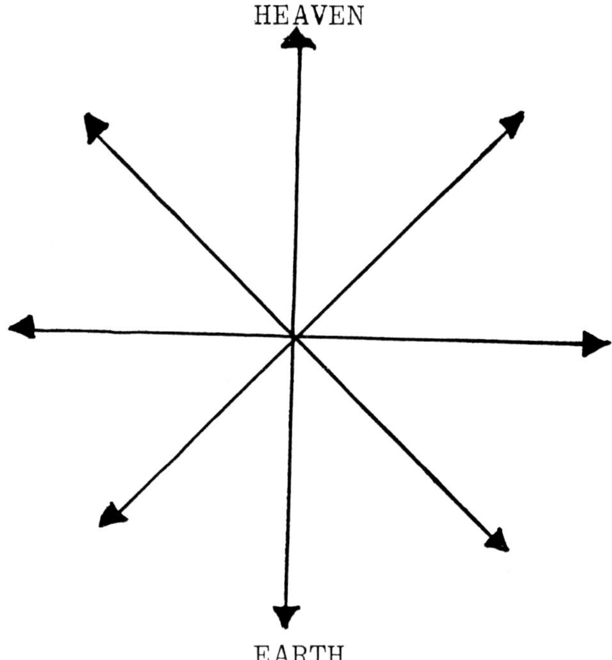

N.B. There are infinite variations according to style and weapon and it is interesting to note that in some systems cuts are named according to where they eminate from and to whence they travel, eg heaven to earth cut = downward blow, whereas earth to heaven would indicate the type of cut used when a sword was drawn by a samurai mounted on horseback. This explains why swords were worn in a particular manner when a samurai was mounted in battle.

An example of two kihon sequences from the following weapons follow:
(1) Roku Shaku Bo

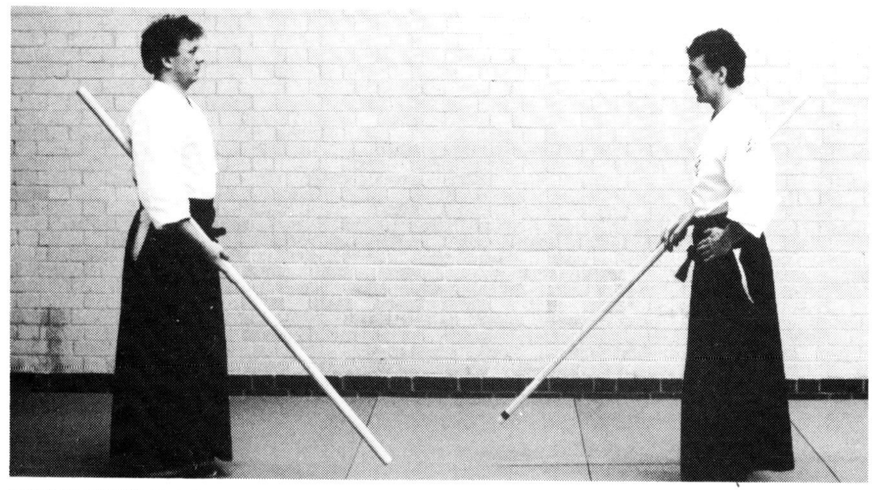

(2) Han-Bo

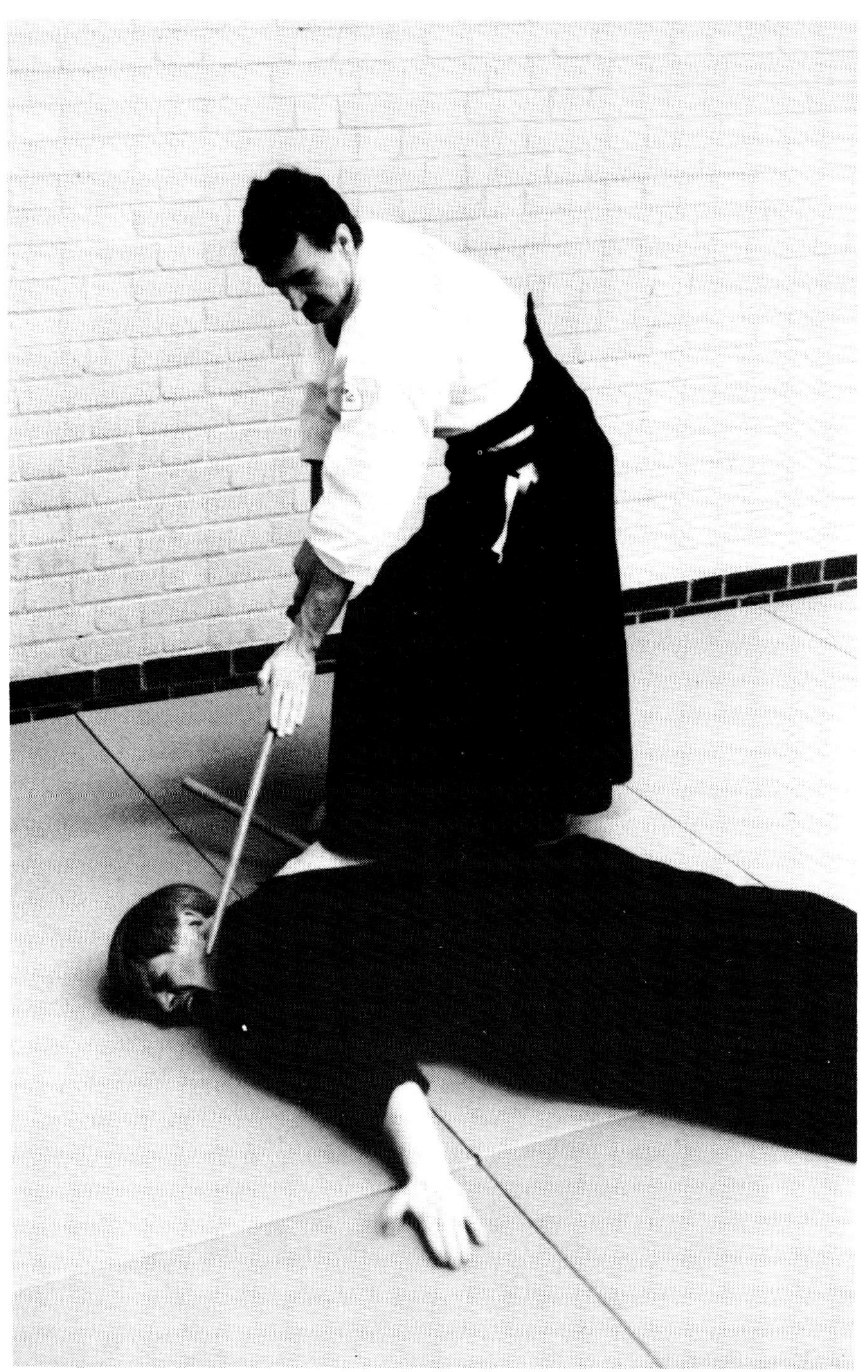

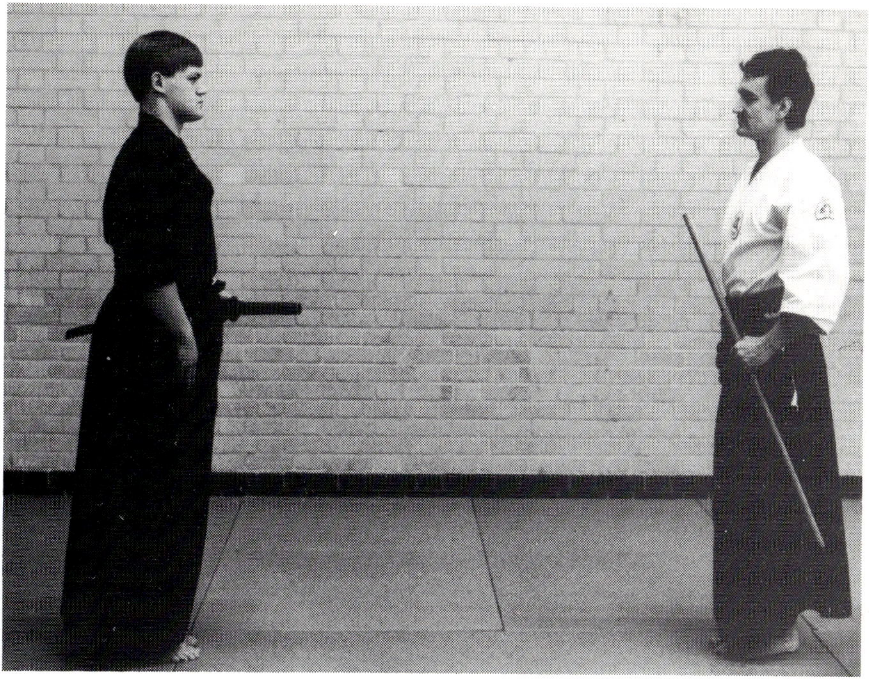

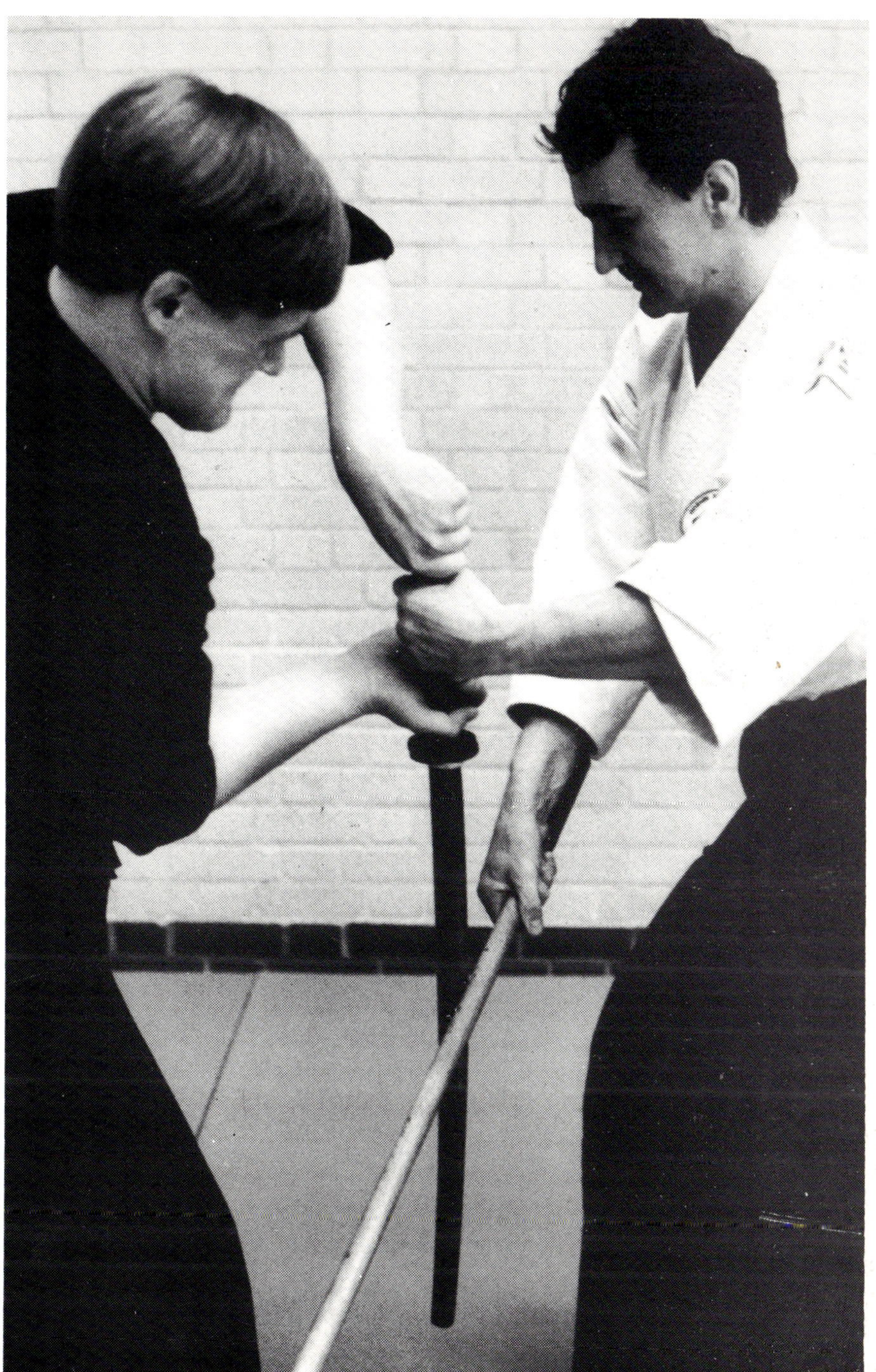

(3) Katana (performed with bokken)

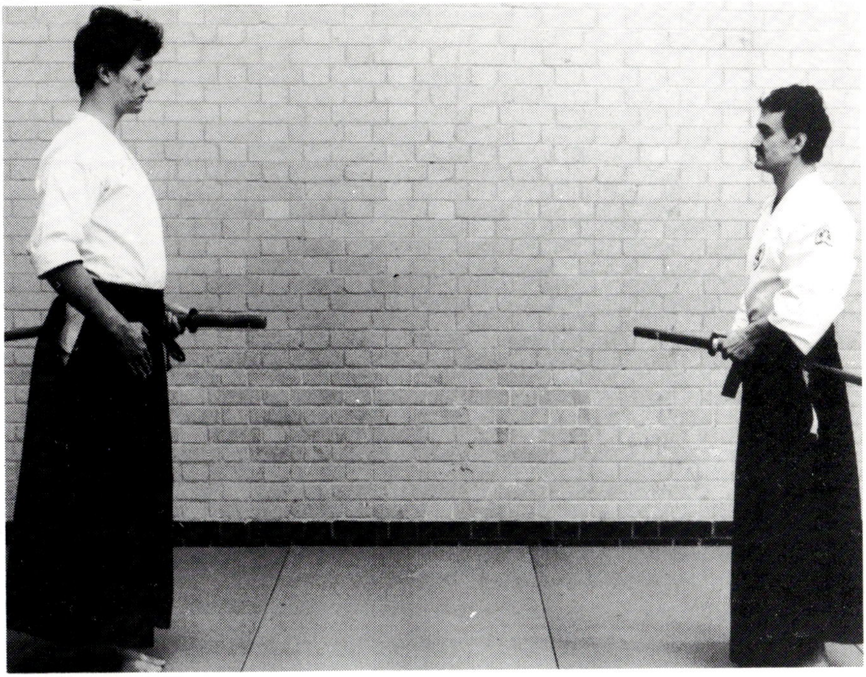

NOTE that the term 'sequence' refers to the starting position of the attack and the block, evasion and counter.

Also mai and zanshin (distancing and awareness) are automatically built into the sequences; as is the correct matters of balance, grip, focus and miscellaneous matters such as the use of the mune and shinogi with particular reference to the katana.

These first two sequences from these particular weapons have been used as S.K. Uyenishi was particularly skilled in these weapons and they are themselves part of the Tenjin Shin Yo Ryu weapons syllabus.

SELF DEFENCE APPLICATION OF KO BUTAN AND TANJO

Practical use of weapons skills against actual assault.

First series of photographs showing one way to evict an individual from a motor vehicle when the window is open but the individual is reluctant to get out under his/her own steam. Note person using Yawara Bo (could be a pen etc) ensures that his own arms and hands are not trapped in the window frame. Never reach too far in as this can leave you open to painful counters.

Second example showing the use of weapons skills in self defence. The defender has used his baton (Tanjo) to lock the antagonist. Note how the offending limb is positioned so as to maximise the effectiveness of the lock. Note also that a preliminary strike is usually (although not always) advisable; this prevents the antagonist tensing up and resisting the lock. On this occassion the preliminary strike was made to the arm itself.

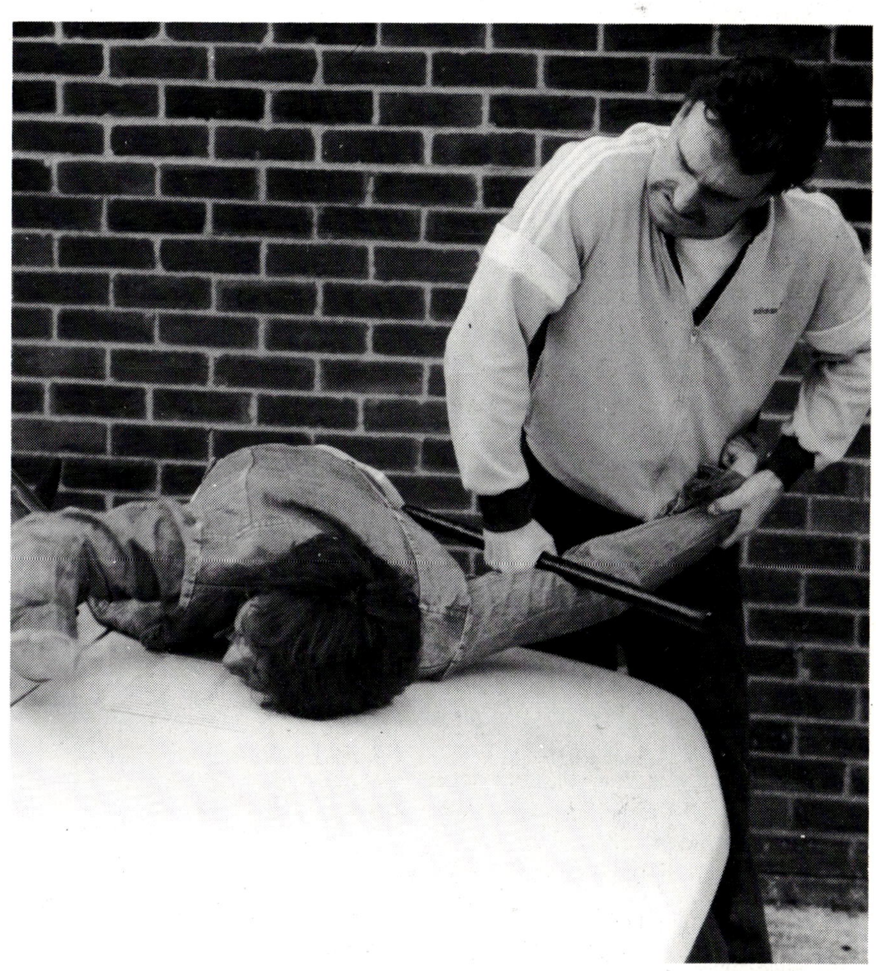

APPENDIX

SPORT BUDO/SPORT JU-JITSU

(Interntional Sport Budo/Sport Ju-Jitsu Federation)

You are about to read through a set of rules which offer a real test of fighting and Martial Skills.

Like any set of rules you must bear in mind that in order to reduce a physical sport into words presents certain difficulties. Complexity may seem a bar to any set of rules. Look, for example, as the rules of cricket or rugby. The rule books are extremely detailed. Yet despite this the respective sports are played and enjoyed by normal folk. Often a seemingly short set of rules appear clear and easy to understand yet they produce problems as whole areas may have been left unresolved. By producing a comprehensive set of rules it is hoped to provide a format which is with a little direction easy to use.

In answer to the inevitable question: "Why a new format when so many already exist?" The answer comes as a result of many years of teaching self defence and close quarter combat skills. When giving seminars on self defence I always ask the following question: "How many of you have been in a real fight?" Having usually a few present who have had real experience I question them further on how the conflict progressed. In the majority of cases the individual concerned states that the fight normally went to very close range or even to ground very quickly. Very few have ever stated that the fight stayed at the range normally associated with Kumite etc. Yet when one opens a magazine on martial arts all the fighters (or at least the majority) have earned their reputation in either Karate, Kick boxing or full contact. No one disputes the fighting spirit and skills needed to succeed in these hard physical formats. Equally, though, all those who practice self defence or work as a doorman or in security will tell you Kumite or sparring skills only form part of the overall fighting skills needed in the street. Therefore sport Budo/Sport Ju-Jitsu provides a format which can be run on a Pentathlon or Triathlon basis and which is equally harsh (if the hardest level of the format is used) to the afforementioned martial forms of Sport contest but which is self defence or combat orientated rather than just Kumite orientated.

Note what follows is a brief introduction etc. The specific rules of each event (either five Pentathlon or three Triathlon events).

It is suggested that you quickly read through these, then read through the scoring explanations.

From the beginning of formal Martial Arts history contesting has taken place. Before the sanctity of life was recognised no holds barred combat allowed the testing of true martial skills and spirit. Many Battlefield developed arts evolved through real experience, by this process of natural selection (Battlefields being no more than large scale contests) techniques were refined and developed.

Sporting contests cannot be seen as the same thing as real conflicts. Real martial arts could only be tested with the rules that the last man or woman left alive or standing is the winner. Such an approach is both morally and practically unacceptable today. Whilst accepting that you cannot turn a real martial art into a sport, one can take certain areas of martial skill and test these in the safety of limited Parameters.

Those who study and teach eclectic, traditional, or composite arts have long required a format which tested those skills associated with such self defence or combat arts, or sciences. "You get good at what you do!" Therefore such practices require an art which tests what they study and is not ruled by aesthetic or other criteria. Sport Budo/Sport Ju Jitsu is such a format. Equally the ultimate test of all round Martial arts ability in the sporting contest. Several different levels of this sport format exist level 1, 2, 3.

Level 1 = Often used for juniors. Light contact used in the free fighting section with strangles allowed in the ground fighting section, and adjudicated rather than allowed to run at refere's discretion. NB safety.

Level 2 = Full contact to the body is used in the free fighting section and a body protection shield may be used, and the groin may be excluded. Sparring contact to head allowed.

Level 3 = Where the full rules as listed apply including the realistic targets in free fighting and the use of full contact to the body and outer thighs. Sparring contact to the head, (or full contact decided at pre tournament meeting) groin always touch contact only, or excluded).

Sport Budo/Sport Ju-Jitsu was developed by Sensei P. J. L. Davies and is developed from the Yawara Ryu Sporting contest format.

International matches have already taken place and an international body governing Sport Budo/Sport Ju-Jitsu is in existence. This is a democratic and amateur body. All those wishing to participate in international or national competitions should contact the Honorary Secretary at the address below:

PART ONE

WEAPONS KIHON. (Section 1)

Player shows a kihon sequence (weapon against weapon) which can be predetermined, utilising any combination of weapons from the following: ROKU SHAKU BO, JO, HANBO, TANJO.

MARKS AWARDED OUT OF 10

BREAKFALLING. (Section 2)

1 minute display including compulsory breakfalls. Marking criteria based on the effectiveness and method of execution.

MARKS AWARDED OUT OF 10

LINE UP OF ATTACKS. (Section 3)

A player is attacked by his own team members (individual entrant is attacked by like entrants). Attacks are indicated to each team member by a referee so that the defending player does not know of the attacks.

Marks are given for vigorous attacking (ensuring attacks are realistic) as well as to the player defending.

MARKS AWARDED FOR DEFENDING OUT OF 8
MARKS AWARDED FOR ATTACKING OUT OF 2

At the end of part one, those players failing to reach required percentages are eliminated: those who succeed in the three areas of part one have their accumulated score carried on and proceed to the 'fighting sections' for competition in the various rounds.

In team matches it is possible to use 10:8:6:2 scoring scenario (as explained in free fighting and ground fighting sections later in text) by means of direct comparison allowing comparison against the 2 direct opponents in each weight division over the 5 events. Alternatively, computation score from part one (1st 3 events) is carried forward to Part 2 favoured for multi round/team tournaments. Scenario to be chosen at pre-tournament meeting.

PART TWO

GROUND FIGHTING. (Section 4)

Players ground fight utilising pressure points, locks and strangles.

FREE FIGHTING. (Section 5)

A vigorous format utilising full contact to the body, touch contact to the head (or full contact in level 3 if decided at pre tournament meeting) and also incorporating the use of throws and locks, allowing the use of realistic targeting and grappling skills.

Player thus competes man to man and obtains a 'fighting' score. This is added to the carry on score and the computation of both provides the winner to proceed to the next round plus accruing points towards their team total overall.

SPORT BUDO/SPORT JU-JITSU

ENTRANTS MUST HAVE: MEDICAL DISCLAIMER, FULL INSURANCE INCLUDING DENTAL COVER

HYGIENE RULES

Persons with cold sores and open cuts will have to wear a dressing over concerning area. If this is not practically possible, the individual will be unable to compete (especially regarding ground fighting section).

Spillages of blood should be attended to by the individual who spilt it (ie, using a strong solution of household bleach) on any mat surface, etc.

Person tending and caring for the individual should ensure that any cuts / open wounds on his/herself are well covered with waterproof dressing/plaster.

Before bouts of ground fighting, hands of both players should be washed in the provided solution of 1 part Milton fluid to 10 parts water and dried using clean paper towels.

Nails should be short and checked, if necessary nail clippers to be used (referee to check).

All scratches and cuts, etc, to be covered by waterproof plaster/dressing.

Removal of any false tooth/teeth.

ETIQUETTE

Traditional etiquette in contest and throughout the tournament to be used.

WEIGHT CATEGORIES

For INTER CLUB matches, the clubs would simply put the best fighters in a numbered order and thus strict weight categories would not have to be complied with unless clubs decided that they preferred to use strict weight divisions.

The weight divisions in tournaments would be as follows: Either or

Either 1 members @ under 65 kilos
2 members @ under 75 kilos (2 to represent widest category re weight)
1 member @ under 85 kilos
1 member @ over 85 kilos

or light weight under 65 kilos
middle weight under 75 kilos
Heavy weight over 75 kilos

These strict weight divisions must be complied with for REGIONAL, NATIONAL and DOMESTIC MERIT TABLES or LEAGUES.

WEIGH IN . . . will take place a minimum of 1 hour before a tournament using an approved accurate set of scales. Referees decision but must comply with the SPORTS BUDO/SPORT JU-JITSU technical committee guidelines.

OUTLINE OF SECTIONS IN DETAIL

WEAPONS KIHON SECTION

This section is to encourage the correct practice of weapons.

Instructors should be aware that by wanting a 'Kihon sequence' the effective and correct use of a weapon will be encouraged.

N.B. Traditional weapons kata in Ju-Jitsu circles predominantly utilised Tori/Uke format rather than solo.

Individual entrants (not in a team) will have to team up with another appropriate entrant in this weapons section and will be allowed to call the attacks clearly; alternatively, they may utilise a non entrant in the contest as their partner, in this section only.

KIHON SEQUENCE may be demonstrated by the following Japanese stick weapons (traditional weapons of many Ju-Jitsu schools):

STICK WEAPONS (single shaft) 6′-2′ in length

—ROKU-SHAKU BO, JO, HAN-BO, TAN-JO

The sequence may be demonstrated weapon against same weapon or any of the named weapons above.

KIHON SEQUENCE must not exceed 2 minutes in duration and may not repeat the same attacks or responses more than three times.

KIHON SEQUENCE should bear relation to the correct uses of that weapon in relation to the traditional Jutsu uses.

Pro forma sheets will be used to assist judges and referees who may only have a basic knowledge of weaponry. However, with support materials and courses run by qualified weaponry personnel, this event may well spread the safe teaching of weaponry from a firm foundation of correct weapon usage.

KIHON must consist of a minimum of 8 separate attacks which are blocked, evaded or countered showing, MA IA and ZANSHIN. (Distancing and awareness.)

BASIC ADJUDICATION FACTORS:
Correct grip of weapon;
Blocking;
Balanced movement and controlled speed.

Players will demonstrate both attacking and defending roles.

Teams will not be penalised for utilising the same sequence as this may be the only weapon they study.

BREAKFALLING SECTION
DURATION OF DISPLAY: 1 minute.
MARKED . . . by way of pro forma schedule.
Following BREAKFALLS are COMPULSORY (marked +)
+ BACK BREAKFALL
+ FORWARD ROLL
+ BACKWARD ROLL
+ SIDE BREAKFALLS (both sides)
+ BACK BREAKFALLS
/ KNEES AND FOREARMS BREAKFALL
+ FRONT BREAKFALL
/ HAND STAND BREAKFALLS
/ FLIP OVERS
(/) optional but can earn extra marks for their difficulty.
N.B.
This display of breakfalling is not a ‘gymnastics’ contest.

Marking criteria reflects Ju-Jitsu self defence application rather than the purely aesthetic considerations.

Other movements may be used to link up the display, however, they will not earn extra marks other than in overall impression.

RANDORI, SELF DEFENCE APPLICATIONS AGAINST ACTUAL ASSAULT

Line up of attackers.

TORI stands inside a square marked on the mat (this square measuring 1 square metre) N.B. when affecting techniques Tori may step out of this area.

Four members of his team (or if an individual entry, four other individual entrants) line up next to a judge.

Judges will quietly tell each attacker the assault / attack that they wish them to execute, on Tori, out of hearing range.

Attackers will attack by rotation, through the line up twice — total 8 attacks. Judges will only deduct marks from Uke for failure to attack realistically and for over reacting to Toris reply, if it was effective in their eyes (Referee discussion, senior referee has deciding role).

Thus, if both attacks are as requested and realistic, player/Uke would keep his two attacking role points (the maximum marks deductable — 2 points).

After this, disqualification for failing to comply with the Referees directions, normal procedure with regards to discipline and non compliance.

All seizures would be executed by attackers raising arms clearly above their own head (this allows Tori to allow one second for Uke to take grip).

When doing seizures, attacker must not execute an assault which entails Tori taking any substantial weight (to avoid back injuries) such as severe pulling backwards or 'jumping up' attacks.

Protective equipment, such as boxes, should be compulsory.

TORI is marked by the Referees using a pro forma marking form.

Marking will be carried out by qualified personnel.

Preferably, one neutral referee and one referee from each competing team to a maximum of five and a minimum of three (always odd numbers).

Locks and atemi finishes must be applied with control (lack of control — discipline rules apply).

The role of TORI is to show effective blocking, evasion, trapping and countering of attacks/assaults.

This may be by way of combination ATEMI WAZA, NAGE WAZA, KATAME WAZA or by any realistic method.

ATEMI or Karate type strikes to correct targets pulled short but with focus, will score equally (as against throwing techniques).

Marks will be deducted from a player who utilises only one method to the exclusion of others, eg, striking as a counter and no throws, or throws only without use of atemi.

A student will not be penalised for repeating a technique if that technique effectively deals with the assault. However, if a player shows a range of techniques combined with effectiveness, he/she may gain extra marks.

The main theme is effective martial techniques and not numerous fancy alternatives.

Pro forma mark sheet attempts to ensure that this primary aim is maintained.

NOTE: Referees must ensure that each defender gets a fair range of appropriate assaults.

GROUND FIGHTING SECTION

WIN . . . by two submissions or through referee stopping the bout on medical grounds, eg, bleeding, etc.

Strict observance of health rules prior to bouts regarding cold sores, cuts, nosebleeds, and hygiene such as referring to gi and nails, etc.

Formal 'bow' etiquette to be followed.

Players must not go higher than up on one foot, alternate knee on the floor. These or equivalent limbs/body must always be in contact with the mat unless grappling makes this impracticable (one opponent on top of the other, etc).

Neither player may stand up/jump attack exerting excessive downward pressure on the other. (Also see restricted techniques below).

RESTRICTED TECHNIQUES

NO attacks against: groin, eyes

NO ripping/pulling/wrenching: nose, ears, mouth/lips, hair
NO head butts, biting or gouging, body slams
NO pressure points applied with finger end.

Use of second knuckle only for applying pressure points (to prevent possible cutting/scratching/bleeding by nails)

NO atemi or kicks/strikes
NO small joint locks (eg fingers/toes) to gain submission.

These may only be utilised as means of affecting an escape from a hold. Any submissions so gained will be seen as invalid.

REFEREE may award a WAZARI where one party is in a dominant position for more than one minute without the other player making any effort to escape (should only be done in cases of extreme inactivity by one player, to a maximum of one point per bout — 1 point = 2 wazari). If one fighter dominates very clearly, referee may award winner 10 points, loser 6 points.

SCORING

Points for a score win or by withdrawal of other player....................10 points
Points for a draw.. 8 points

Points for a close loss (within and including one point)..................... 6 points
Points for completing the two minutes and losing.......................... 2 points

ADJUDICATION OF STRANGLES
If a referee stops a fight because he sees a strangle causing unconsciousness, he must consult other referees as to whether they agree that it would have been decisive.

If any dispute, the referee may award a WAZARI instead of an IPPON — at the referees discretion.

A referee can also utilise a warning and a score deduction against a player who fails to comply with the contesting rules or who uses illegal / disallowed techniques (same as in other sections):
1st warning...Ippon deducted
2nd warning.......................................disqualified (eg, lose the bout)

N.B. Refereeing by way of Minor System (one high one low) working alternate L's.

FREE FIGHTING SECTION
Continuous clicker type Knockdown format
EQUIPMENT
NB if level 3 is used 'safe gloves' of a standard type must be used by all competitors. (for full contact 8 or 10oz gloves are recommended)
Approved mits, shin and instep pads approved kick boots, elbow pads;
Gum shield;

Breast protectors for lady entrants;

Boxes should be worn on the outside of the gi, alternative colour to gi pants to show a clear target for referee and judges.

Full boxer shatterproof protector also advised to be worn under gi pants (not compulsory).

Body protectors may be worn but only approved type (decision about use will rest with the Sport Budo/Sport Ju-Jitsu technical committee, depending on what level of Sport Budo/Sport Ju-Jitsu is being used.

DURATION
One continuous bout lasting 3 minutes.

SCORING
PRIMARY TARGETS
Head, side of neck, light, medium contact (see below), the groin must always be touch only.

Blows to these areas must be light or medium sparring contact, defined as light or medium force normally associated with prefight boxing sparring (unless full contact level 3 when touch contact to groin, or excluded). Light enough to minimise the risk of brain damage, heavy enough to teach realism.

Control must be shown but good focus and ma ia also.
(NB level 3 may be full contact to head. Decided at pre tournament meeting).
Blows struck successfully to these PRIMARY TARGETS score.......IPPON
If the target is struck with lack of focus or without good balance..WAZARI
If attacked individual evades or rides the blow.........................WAZARI

NON PRIMARY OR SECONDARY TARGETS
Front of body above the belt as in boxing, torso, outer side of thighs. These non primary targets do not usually score except in Junior level one format matches when they are equal $\frac{1}{4}$ point. In level two and three they only score if a knockdown takes place. It is possible, however, if Pre Tournament Committees wish to score body when level two is used. Level three format is always knockdown, or full contact.

NB. SAFETY REGARDING KNEES AND ELBOWS
(always excluded from back)
Also maybe excluded from use if agreed (at pre-tournament meeting) must be touch contact only to head (full contact to body except lower stomach and heart). Full harsh, or medium to head can be used by prior arrangement but touch contact, etc, would normally be for youngsters or veterans' contests.

Knees and elbows would be excluded in level one matches (juniors) as can the groin as a target (otherwise decided at pre tournament meeting).

OUT OF BOUNDS AREAS: (SHADED AREAS)
NO: finger strikes to eyes, ears.
NO: head butts, biting, pinching, spitting, tearing/wrenching, hair pulling.
NO: linear kicks to the legs, kicks under the groin, descending elbows to head knees and elbows must be used with control medium contest also to the torso.

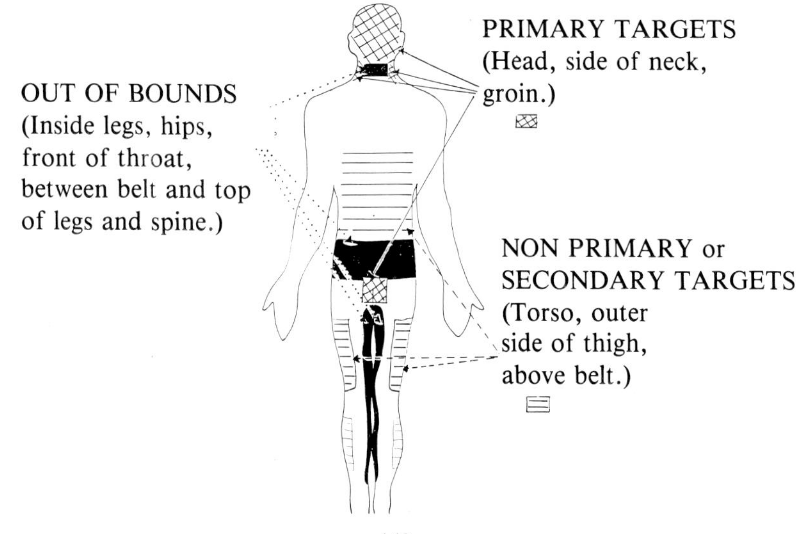

ADVANTAGE PERIOD IN THE FREE FIGHTING (NB in full contact senario 5 seconds grappling period allowed)

Real conflicts require a quick and forceful response. If one reads the rules through in the free fighting section one can see how the referees discretion with regards to this section is of paramount importance.

The logic behind the rule relates to the real world's self defence situation. If Tori hits in the groin, neck or side of head it would sufficiently distract Uke thus allowing him to complete a throw or other finish. Equally if Tori threw Uke to the ground in the real world, the hard impact on landing would distract Uke sufficiently to make it unlikely that Uke would counter. In order for the free fighting advantage period to be realistic the referee must ensure that if Tori strikes a primary target and looks likely to go on to throw, the extra 5 second advantage period is allowed to run. If Tori then throws Uke the referee can allow the second advantage period on the floor for Tori to be able to further amass his score.

If Tori or Uke strike a primary target but it is obvious in the referee's opinion that the player scoring on primary target is unlikely to be able to take advantage he just calls break. (E.g., if Tori scored with a roundhouse kick to Uke's head and Uke was about to execute a throw after the kick scored, the referee may call break thus Tori scores without undue punishment when the advantage should be running for Tori.)

RESTRICTED TECHNIQUES SUPPLEMENTARY

NO: Attack initiated by a jumping up movement where attacked individual supports full weight of antagonist on his neck or back.

NO: Body slams or picking up techniques unless person lowered in a controlled manner.

NO: Take down delivering blows to the back, eg, back-breaks.

NO: Wrenching techniques.

Cautions exercised on the basis of excessive contact to a primary target, etc, or for dissent of any offence connected with the tournament:

1st Warning.................................IPPON deducted
2nd Warning...Disqualified

ALL BOUTS MUST BE STRICTLY REFEREED AND REFEREES MUST BE AWARE OF INDIVIDUALS

(a) Faking injury (b) Over responding

ADJUDICATION RULES

Minimum of: 1 referee, 3 judges, 1 scorekeeper, per matted area.

ATTIRE TO BE WORN

REFEREE

Formal grey slacks, socked feet (white, grey or blue only) blazer or very smart jumper with Sport Budo logo (Navy/Black).

JUDGES/SCOREKEEPER/TIMEKEEPER

As above except if off the matted area — white soled training shoes may be worn, or zori.

For striking a primary target as indicated in chart, = ippon (one point).

(Side of head, back of head, face, neck side and back (not front of throat).)

Groin = IPPON (one point)

For a clean throw = 3 points

For a take down = 2 points

For a messy or indecisive throw = ippon (one point)

For a knock down by blow to legal secondary target for a count of five or more = 3 points.

For a knock down by legal blow to secondary targets for more than ten seconds = knockout.

If a full contact to head is used knockout 10 seconds counts.

For a lock or strangle executed either in grappling epoch or ground epoch by player for whom the advantage period is running technical knockout (lock on indicated by submission (tapping)), or Lock put on when advantage period is open that is not running in anyone's favour.

CONTACT DEFINED

Primary targets excluding groin. Medium to light contact. The force should be such that is is unlikely to cause brain damage or if level 3, harsh sparring or full contact decided at pre tournament meeting.

KNOCK DOWN JIUDO

A grappling and striking format suitable for well prepared students.

OBLIGATORY EQUIPMENT

Box, strong traditional plain gi tied with a belt.

Target areas for blows and kicks;

Above the belt and below the neck; The body front (Torso) and the top outside edge of the thighs.

RESTRICTED TECHNIQUES

No blows to the head at all (unless pre arranged by players and referee with touch contact only and referees awarding either full or half points according to focus etc).

No blows directly aimed at the heart, this area to be shown by positioning of club badge on the gi jacket.

SCORING

Clean throw = IPPON — one point

Scrappy throw = WAZARI — half point

Knockdown = (under five seconds) = 2 × IPPON (Two Points)

Knockdown = (over five seconds) = IPPON

Knockout = If knocked down and unable to continue after fifteen seconds.

N.B. After a knockdown a compulsary count of 10 seconds must be imposed before player can continue referees ensuring he or she is fit to continue.

Refereeing by any of two referees working in "Mirror Format" patrolling the opposite L's of the fight area.

BOUTS DURATION

Either by pre arranged time limit e.g. 3 minutes or the first to set score, say three points.

NB The Option to continue down to the ground where a submission would count as a knockout can also be included but in order that Judo; Ju Jitsu; Kempo and knockdown karate men can compete on an equal footing this is usually not included unless by prior arrangement.